WOMEN TO WOMEN

To MUM

For your courage, love, and faithfulness—
against so many odds

Women
to
Women

Edited by
Kathy Keay

MARC
Evangelical Alliance

British Library Cataloguing in Publication Data

Keay, Kathy
  Women to women: good news for women . . .
  1. Women in Christianity
  I. Title
  262′.15   BV639.W7

  ISBN 0-86065-625-X

Unless otherwise noted, Scripture quotations in this publication are from the Holy Bible, New International Version. Copyright © 1973, 1978, 1984, International Bible Society. Published in Britain by Hodder and Stoughton. Used by permission.

Contents

Part II: One to Another

Part III: Resources

Foreword

One of the most remarkable things about Jesus is that he was not interested in hearing what the men of his day thought about women. Instead he gave women space to be themselves and, in a very real sense, to tell their own stories. His mind was not influenced by the pronouncements of the religious authorities or the legal experts, or even of his own disciples. He made up his own mind about the woman taken in adultery, the woman who anointed him with oil and washed his feet with her tears, the woman who sat and listened rather than waiting on him, the outcast woman at the well, the poor widow, the Cyro-Phoenician woman. His empathy is all the more remarkable because it is in stark contrast to the dismissive, often humiliating, attitudes of those around him.

Women, then, were to tell their own stories. For it was to women that the greatest story of all time was entrusted: the women who had watched as their dearest friend was put to death unjustly, and who had now come to sweeten his corpse. They have told the story well. Now we know it, too; we know that nobody was there, but that Christ is risen. Yet even when that story was first told by the women, it was dismissed by the disciples as nonsense.

We all need space, then, to tell our stories and to find those who will listen. The lives of ordinary people are important, whether they are men or women. Their stories give us a glimpse of what it is to be human, what it means to be sad or lonely or exhilarant or triumphant. They lead us closer to understanding the message of the cross: salvation, reconciliation and love. For we are the people for whom Christ died—we with our ordinary lives and our ordinary hurts, problems and joys.

So let these women tell their stories and share their ideas, and let us read them with openness, gentleness and sensitivity. Kathy Keay helps women discover their identities as Christians and as bearers of Good News.

Elaine Storkey

Commendation

Women to Women shows women on many different spiritual journeys. What they have all discovered, though, is that they cannot travel alone: they need to draw together—sometimes away from the demands of work and family—to share common experiences and to receive support and understanding. Thus after we read the accounts of women who have reached out to other women in constructive ways with the Gospel of Christ, we then read of practical ways women can make such groups work.

We are delighted that Kathy Keay and the other contributors have offered us ways of preaching the Good News in a world divided too often along sexual lines. This book will have wide-ranging gospel significance.

David Cohen, Scripture Union
Marlene Cohen, Southwark Diocese

Acknowledgements

Anita Hydes' full story, *Snatched from the Flames*, is published by Kingsway and written by Tony Ralls.

Sue Barnett has written a book on spiritual fitness called *Fit for a King*, published by Kingsway.

'It Was a Woman' first appeared in the Tasmanian Mothers' Union Newsletter, also in the Australian Mothers' Union magazine, *Mia Mia*. Accompanying line drawing by Susan Colman of the English Mothers' Union magazine, *Home and Family*. Both used by kind permission.

Material in the chapter on reaching feminists first appeared in an article on feminism in *Christian Woman* magazine, and has been used with permission.

Charts in 'Single Parent Families' kindly supplied by One Parent Families from its 1986 Annual Report.

Ethne Mason's letter in the Christian Viewpoint chapter reproduced here by permission of *Christian Viewpoint* magazine.

Anne Cooper is grateful to Margaret Wardell and to a number of other friends, both Asian and British, for sharing their experiences with her.

The material in Part Two on women's groups, discussion groups, and sexual abuse counselling first appeared in the 'Men Women and God' information pack and has been adapted and used with permission.

The 'Double-Sided Debate' is reprinted with permission of the Department of Mission of the Baptist Union of Great

Britain and Ireland from *Free Indeed?*

The sketches 'God and Man and Woman' and 'He and She' have been used with permission from *Wild Goose Prints: Sketches from the Iona Community*, Wild Goose Publications, by John Bell and Graham Maule, also 'Touching Place'.

I would particularly like to thank all the women who have talked so openly about their faith and the lack of it, on buses and trains, on organised missions and in homes. Thanks, too, to all my worker friends and co-travellers from UCCF who are now serving God as a result, mainly overseas, especially Tricia Perkins in Southern Africa, and Claire Evans in Thailand. A special thank you to Lynn Summers for her encouragement in the early stages, to Di Kerton and Carol Morris. Carol became a Christian during the writing of this book. Thank you too for the encouragement of Janet Morgan, Elaine Storkey, Faith and Roger Forster, and for the example of Sue Brown and Sharon Anson who have boldly gone where few women have gone before. Special thanks to Lizzie Gibson for her encouragement and professional skills in the joint editorial process.

Kathy Keay

Preface

Jesus said, 'I have come that they may have life, and have it to the full.' (John 10:10)

'All things are yours ... the world or life or death or the present or the future—all are yours, and you are of Christ, and Christ is of God.' (I Cor. 3:21–23)

> To the lost Christ shows his face
> to the unloved he gives his embrace
> to those who cry in pain or disgrace
> Christ makes with his friends a touching place.

> (*Touching Place*, The Wild Goose Worship Group
> Iona Community)

PART I

OUR STORIES

It Was A Woman

It was a woman
who watched over her little brother
when he was hidden in the bulrushes —

It was a woman
who urged her father to perform his vow,
although her own life might be sacrificed.

It was a woman
who so beautifully said 'All was well'
when she came to implore the prophet to restore
her dead and only son.

It was a woman
who followed her mother-in-law
in all her distress and poverty.

It was a woman
who offered her last mite in charity.

It was a woman
who washed our blessed Saviour's feet with her tears
and afterwards wiped them with her hair.

It was a woman
who said, 'Lord, if you hadst been here,
my brother had not died!'

It was a woman
who stood at the foot of the Cross.

It was a woman
who went first to the sepulchre.

It was to a woman
our Lord first made himself known
after his resurrection.

From Tasmanian MU Newsletter

1. Introduction

The Gospel of Jesus has always been Good News to women. Yet increasing numbers find it hard to identify with our churches, when even the language that is used so often excludes them.

What can we say to women whom the Church is failing to reach, and how can we go about communicating the Good News of the Gospel to them? The traditional women's meeting is no longer relevant to more than a few. Women's lifestyles and commitments vary so widely today that one meeting is unlikely to cater for them all. The women who have written these chapters recognise in different ways that women have a particular responsibility to reach out to other women with the love of Christ. They have all broken into unknown territory, often in fear and trembling, but knowing that God has called them to reach out to other women in new and imaginative ways. Part One tells their stories. Each brings with it an understanding and identification with specific groups of women: the single parent, the mother at home, the professional woman, as well as those who are easily forgotten: women in prison, Asian and West Indian women, feminists, young, isolated women and the elderly. It also includes the story of one woman who has the chance to witness in a rather unusual way, through the professional world of golf. And this is by no means a comprehensive list; there are many women who work as evangelists, though not specifically among women, who also have their stories to tell. I hope this book will encourage them to do so.

It is certainly time that we recovered our legacy, given first to Mary on Easter day, to 'Go and tell'. It doesn't take great expertise, only a willingness to share what each of us knows about the reality of God in our lives, and to identify with the particular pains and struggles in the lives of the women we meet.

A survey conducted among women in London in 1984 identified five main issues of female concern: the fear of rape and/or sexual abuse, loneliness, problems related to bringing up children alone, family, and financial difficulties. Add to this unemployment, housing problems, unwanted pregnancies, sickness and broken relationships, and you have a fairly accurate picture of the mosaic of many womens' lives. Even among middle-class women, there are many who may give the appearance that all is well, but who may also be living lives of quiet desperation.

No book on Christianity and Women would be complete without a section on Jesus' attitude to women. So the book begins here. In Paul's letter to the Galatians, we read that when the time had fully come, God sent his Son, born of a woman, born under law, to redeem those under law (Gal. 4:4–5). In Jesus' time, few people were more bound by that law than women. This is still very much the case the world over. Wherever we are, Jesus comes to liberate women from sin and all that binds them, particularly from traditional expectations and stereotypes that prevent us from being all we were meant to be. A living personal faith in Christ has helped many women to live through difficult and often unchanging circumstances, where otherwise there would be little hope.

There is no limit to what can be done through a life which is open to God's leading and available to others. And there is rarely an ideal time to begin, whatever lifestyle we lead. During the production of this book many of the contributors went through major changes in their own lives and in some cases the lives of their families. One woman struggled through morning sickness and the early stages of pregnancy when writing her chapter; two others had to move house. Some sections were written in between work shifts and looking after families; one contributor wrote her chapter during a relapse of multiple sclerosis, and another stepped in at the last minute to relieve someone whose husband had just been diagnosed as having cancer of the liver.

Not all the contributors are well known, as it is not only the famous, courageous women who will be remembered for their faithful witness and good deeds. The woman who poured ointment over Jesus's feet was told that her story would be told from generation to generation, because she had loved much. There are hundreds of similar acts of love and mercy which are waiting to be done for women and by women in the name of Christ. I hope that you and I will also play our parts.

The women who first saw the risen Christ have paved the way for us. Let us follow their example, gaining strength from one another.

Kathy Keay

2. Jesus and Women

Many women have said to me, 'I couldn't possibly become a Christian—Christianity is so male dominated.' When we look at the Church, this may still be so; but when we look at the gospels they are filled with stories of Jesus' encounters with women. Luke's gospel, especially, reminds us that at the heart of the Christian faith is a God who has time for women. Nearly one-third of the material in Luke deals directly with women; in fact, as far back as 1896 a New Testament scholar, Alfred Plummer, called it 'the gospel of Womanhood'. Women who want to be sure that Christianity will be real for them need only look at this gospel to be reassured. Women who don't particularly want to be religious, but who want a genuine relationship with God, will also—I believe—be inspired as they read this gospel. Likewise those who admit to being hurt and disappointed by men find in Jesus, both man and God, one who can not only heal old wounds, but restore confidence in relationships between the sexes.

Jesus didn't fall into the trap of loving only beautiful women. He could see what made a woman tick, and this wasn't always in keeping with traditional roles. Jesus affirmed each woman he met as unique and special—and still does today. Whether she is single or married, bearing children or not, Jesus offers new life, hope, healing and a new experience of intimacy in relationships, which most women long for.

To be a woman, then, is not to be inferior or second-class, no matter what others may have made us feel. In the eyes of Jesus, men are not more important because they may be more educated or earn the money or have a more direct calling from God; women are equally valued by him—created equal in his image (Gen. 1), given equal responsibility to steward the earth's resources (Gen. 1:28); women are equally responsible for the fall (Gen. 3), and equal heirs of salvation through Jesus (Gal. 3:28).

The Good News for women today in a highly self-conscious, sex-orientated world is that in Christ 'there is neither Jew nor Greek, slave nor free, male nor female' (Gal. 3:28); in other words, all that women feel which disadvantages them one way or another in Christ has no weight at all. We need to encourage one another to believe that when our identity is rooted securely in him, then it is possible to stand firm, even when we feel weighed down, treated badly, taken for granted or simply ignored.

Jesus draws on women's experience many times to illustrate something about the Kingdom of God. In this respect his parables were quite unconventional in their time. Just as a man who plants mustard seed reveals something of this, so does a woman who makes bread; those who persevere in prayer are compared to a friend who wakes his neighbour at night, and a woman who succeeds in obtaining a hearing with the judge—not an easy thing for a woman to do either then or now! The nature of God is illustrated in the parable of a shepherd who searches for one lost sheep, and of the woman who searches for the one lost coin. There is no doubt that Jesus in his ministry touched and empowered women every bit as much as he did men.

Jesus scandalised those around him by affirming the gifts and identity of women—even those who were thought to be unclean: he showed no prejudice towards the ritually unclean, whether women or men. He drank from the cup of a Samaritan woman (John 4:1); he welcomed the faith of a haemorrhaging woman who reached out to touch him

(Luke 8:40–47); he refused to rebuke the woman who burst into Simon the Pharisee's house and lavished kisses upon him (Luke 7:36–50); and he declared that prostitutes understood more about the nature of the Kingdom than many men learned in the Law (Matt. 21:31–32). On these occasions and many more, we see Jesus welcoming women in a way that was completely unheard-of by the religious people of his day. At every point he defended women as people, living out the instruction later given to Peter: 'Do not call anything impure that God has made clean.' (Acts 10:15) These encounters with women can be referred to when we talk to women with problems that are long-term and not necessarily easy to solve.

Women with Health Problems

Most women at some time in their lives have to cope with health problems, many of which are related specifically to their being female. If you are a woman, no doubt you will know only too well what I mean! How many times at work or at home have people said 'Oh, don't take any notice of so-and-so, it's the time of the month,' or, 'She's got PMT.' I have a friend who reckons that the reason her marriage split up was because her husband was convinced that she was always either pre-menstrual, menstrual or post-menstrual—in other words, there was no time at all when he felt he could communicate with her on an equal level as a human being who was not in some way influenced by her monthly cycle! Jesus refused to define women in this way.

Instead, his response to the woman with the issue of blood in Luke 8 is really liberating for women who struggle with gynaecological health problems. This old woman had been ill for over 12 years. She not only bore the pain of constant haemorrhaging, but also the disgrace of knowing herself to be unclean in the eyes of the Law. After 12 long years she had every reason to believe that hope had gone. No doctor could help her. She only grew worse under their care, and her savings had all been used in search of medical relief. Imagine the scene: this woman, who was no doubt smelly and in every way untouchable, hid in the crowd that followed Jesus. She had seen Jairus (before whom the powerful bowed) fall at Jesus' feet and beg for assistance. There was no one like Jairus to plead her case; how could she dare to ask for herself? She was no Jairus; she was not even the daughter of a Jairus. She was just a poor anonymous woman carrying her pain deep within—suffering, but with no voice. As Jesus drew near, she touched him very slightly—a simple gesture of reaching and receiving. Immediately she knew the flow of blood had ceased.

'Who touched me?' said Jesus. The disciples must have thought he was mad as hordes of people pressed against him. Yet Jesus searched the faces of the people.

'Someone touched me; I know that power has gone out from me,' he said. Imagine how the woman must have felt. She came forward, falling down as Jairus had, telling Jesus everything. She hadn't meant to interrupt his journey. There was no hint of dismay in Jesus, no suggestion that her touch made him unclean. He listened to her story. 'Daughter, your faith has healed you. Go in peace,' he said. In calling her 'daughter'—an intimate and affectionate term—her rightful place was re-established in the community. From being a woman who had been cut off and an outcast, she was not only healed physically but restored socially to her own people, among whom she belonged. Jesus had declared that this woman was precious. In his eyes, she wasn't just an outcast—a woman with incurable medical problems—she was somebody unique, worth listening to and caring for, and he commended her for her courageous faith. Reaching out, touching, receiving a new name and departing with a quiet sense of dignity: this cycle has been the experience of other women, too, who have reached out to Jesus in the midst of the loneliness of their pain.

I once went to an art gallery in Brixton where women's experience of hospitals was portrayed through poems, diaries and paintings. Each communicated a feeling of aloneness, anger and the waste of hours spent in waiting rooms and hospital beds. These women resented being treated like cattle—prodded and poked and longing to shout out as one woman did, 'Hey, this is me you're poking!'

There is nothing in the gospel accounts to support a holier-than-thou attitude towards being a Christian. Jesus didn't come just to 'save souls', as we sometimes hear, but through the process of salvation and redemption to make us whole people. This is particularly important for women, who for much of their lives are especially conscious of the body, its rhythms and demands, particularly during pregnancy and early motherhood. The story of Jesus and the woman with the issue of blood is significant for women who have gynaecological problems. Healing may not always be instant; but encountering Jesus, with mind, body and soul makes us open to his healing power in every area of our lives—healing which, though slow in its working, may be real nevertheless and has been experienced by many.

The Childless

Jesus not only violated the distinctions between clean and unclean; he also challenged the common view that bearing children, especially sons, was the fulfilment of a woman's life. The absence of children was considered a great misfortune for a woman, at times even interpreted as divine punishment. A fruitful womb was a sign of God's blessing; the barren womb was seen as a curse.

One day, as Jesus was teaching, a woman cried out from the crowds: 'Blessed is the mother who gave you birth and nursed you.' (Luke 11:27–28). Presumably this woman intended to compliment Jesus. He did not refuse the compliment, but his response shows that he saw her statement as inadequate. He used the situation to challenge the woman to a deeper faith: 'Blessed rather are those who hear the word of God and obey it.' Jesus says in effect, that it is not a woman's womb (not even his mother Mary's) which is her source of true blessedness, but her response to the word of God. New creation by the Word, not procreation by the womb, is the fulfilment of what it means to be a woman.

Every woman—whether married with children, married without children, single, divorced with or without children, or engaged—needs to take this teaching very much to heart.

Women and Theology

It is difficult for us today to understand how radical it was for Jesus to call women to follow him as disciples. Women in his day were not considered candidates for discipleship by rabbis! Nevertheless, it is clear that women were among those who followed Jesus through cities and villages, bringing the Good News of the Kingdom of God (Luke 8:1–3). Luke provides us with the names of some of these women: Joanna, Susanna and Mary called Magdalene. The seclusion of home and the roles of daughter, wife and mother, which were (and still are to many women) confining, were confronted by the uncompromising call of Jesus. Just as Peter left his nets, women such as Joanna left their assigned roles and took up the transient lifestyle of their teacher. This may come as a shock to us today, when so much emphasis is placed on family life and the importance of women at home. Those who have left family responsibilities in order to live for a higher cause (for example the women of Greenham Common), are regarded with suspicion, seen to have deserted their families, generally regarded as outcasts.

This was not so in Jesus' time, when the community took more of a corporate responsibility for the bringing up of children, so that even if a parent was absent, members of the household, especially the young, would rarely be left alone and uncared for.

The story of Mary and Martha (Luke 10) is well known to most of us and superbly parodied in Jill Tweedy's *Letters from a Faint-Hearted Feminist*. Most of us at one time or another have had a clear sense that we are either a Mary or a Martha, and the gulf between the two women still exists in the Church and world today. Yet Jesus loved both women, challenging and affirming them in different ways. The story always appears hard on Martha and on those women who struggle with the common task and daily round, often caught in a treadmill at home with the demands of their families. Jesus had something to say to Martha then, and he still does to the Marthas of today. While Martha was busy serving the guests, Mary we are told 'sat at the Lord's feet and listened to his teaching'. The term 'sitting at the feet' of another describes the attentive listening and learning of disciple with teacher. Paul speaks of himself as one who 'sat at the feet of Gamaliel' (Acts 22:3). This was extremely unusual for a woman in Jesus' time, and even today women who study theology rather than perhaps getting married and running a home are seen by some as 'unfeminine', perhaps even not quite 'real women', 'sublimating' their femininity.

Martha, irritated that her sister was not helping to serve, asked Jesus to scold Mary for failing to lend a hand. Yet Jesus refused to do this. Rather, he insisted that Mary had a right to the place she had chosen. 'Mary has chosen what is better, and it will not be taken away from her,' he says (Luke 10:42).

This does not mean that women whose primary responsibilities lie within the home should feel second-class citizens, as is so easily the case today; rather, that they should hear the challenge of Jesus, to make time to sit at his feet and learn from him—even amidst all the demands of everyday life.

Single women in particular who choose a non-domestic lifestyle and who love the Lord are often made to feel that their very femininity is being challenged. A new neighbour suggested recently to a friend of mine that she couldn't possibly like living alone. She asked her if she could cook, and why she had moved to her new home alone. In a new town development where most of the women have young families perhaps this did seem a bit odd, but in Jesus' eyes her lifestyle is as valid as any, and not to be despised.

Breaking Through Cultural Barriers

Later in this book are chapters relating to communication with women from different cultural backgrounds. It is easy for all of us to stay within the confines of that which we find familiar. However, Jesus' encounter with the Samaritan woman (John 4) challenges all of us to reach out to women from other backgrounds, even if this means breaking through racial and cultural barriers that are recognised worldwide. The Jews and Samaritans had long been at war with each other. And as a woman, the Samaritan knew that it was not up to her to initiate conversation. Much to her surprise, Jesus, the Jew, was the one to reach out to her. The chance meeting at the well—as it seemed—developed into a woman's encounter with Jesus that was to lead her to salvation. They spoke about Jacob's Well, about her life, about worship and about the One who was to come. As in many conversations about faith, there seemed to be all kinds of 'red herrings', but Jesus always brought her back to the main issues. There were her own spiritual needs, and the fact that these could be more than adequately met through Christ. Imagine what she must have felt as Jesus made it clear that he knew all about her life! She had not only no husband, but had lived with five other men—and he knew it. Yet Jesus did not condemn. Rather, by describing her circumstances bluntly, he invited her to challenge her search for intimacy and to find it in a Source that would not leave her disappointed.

So many women today desperately need to drink from the living water which Jesus gives. Since the so-called sexual liberation of the sixties, many women have gone from man to man searching for intimacy and security, a search which has frequently left them worse off than before. Jo, a friend of mine who has recently had an abortion, with one child already conceived out of marriage, admitted that she could never imagine herself within a stable marriage. 'It seems likely that I'll go from one tumultuous relationship to another,' she said. 'It's tough, but I just can't see any way out of it.' For women like this—and many others—Jesus invites them, saying, 'If any one thirst, let her come to me and drink.'

It is easy to condemn those who are seemingly promiscuous. In fact the pressures of sticking with a Christian marriage can make this condemnation even more easy. Why should other women be allowed to roam fancy-free, when I'm stuck here with the kids, the washing up, piles of dirty clothes and an endless routine!

All of us need to realise that at the heart of *every* person's experience is a void which only the Lord Jesus can fill. Unless we believe this, we will never get beyond being able to relate only to women whose circumstances are like ours, good though this may be. Yet if we believe that God loves each woman whom we meet and with whom we form a friendship—no matter how tenuous—we can learn to introduce her gradually and sensitively to the Source of living water, who can both create and quench her inner thirst.

At the end of the story of Jesus's encounter with the Samaritan woman, we are told that she ran into the city, telling people about Jesus, and many believed because of her testimony. It is often through the lives of those who seem least open to Christ that others are most convinced when they do eventually become Christians.

The different pictures of women in the gospels shine out as proof for all time that there is no woman too insignificant to be of value to Christ and his Kingdom.

Women and Poverty

Of all the world's poor, we find in practically every country that women are among those who suffer most. This is not just the case in developing countries, or during times of famine, when women tend to feed their husband and families first, but also in Western cultures where the divide between rich and poor is becoming increasingly great. As jobs become harder to find for the so-called unskilled, and benefits are cut, women in our own society find it difficult to make ends meet. The single parent, the widow—even the divorced clergy wife—all are made vulnerable in a society where money and power are heavily linked. The story of the widow's gift in Luke 21 is especially significant here. Jesus watched everyone enter the synagogue. One after another they placed their gift into the plate, and he knew them each by heart: their lives, visible to all, as well as what was secret and hidden. In sharp contrast, a widow came in, shabbily dressed no doubt, and looking very insignificant. She placed her contribution into the plate. Yet out of all of those who went before her, Jesus knew that she had given not out of her wealth, but out of her poverty. Her gift was small, but she gave everything she had. Such wholehearted devotion will never go unnoticed in God's eyes. No matter what our circumstances and however low our funds, a generous heart, and complete, revered devotion to Christ, especially in the midst of the struggle with poverty, will not be easy but will have its own unmistakable rewards.

Luke tells the story of how Jesus raised the widow's son. It is a beautiful story of how Jesus recognises the unique pain of the bereaved, especially if they are already alone and socially vulnerable. This happened when Jesus was on his way to a town called Nain, accompanied by his disciples and a large crowd who came with him. As he approached the town gate, the dead person was being carried out—the only son of his mother, a widow. Imagine the scene: a large crowd from the town was with her. She was surrounded by people, yet she must have felt terribly lonely inside and destitute after the loss of her husband and son, especially in a society where women had no legal nor social standing beyond their kinsmen. When Jesus saw her, we are told that 'his heart went out to her and he said, "Don't cry."' (Luke

7:13) It seems a strange thing for him to say to anyone in those circumstances, especially when he himself wept at the grave of Lazarus and cried over Jerusalem. What did he mean, then, when he said to the widow 'Don't cry'? The story tells of how he went and touched the coffin, amazing those who stood around him. He simply said to the one inside, 'Young man, I say to you, get up!' As Jesus spoke, the dead man sat up and began to talk. We are not told what he said, only that Jesus must have taken him by the hand and given him back to his mother.

Now, many of us can testify that although this was indeed a miracle, it is not usually the case that when we lose loved ones, they are restored immediately to us. One of the points of the story here is rather that when we suffer bereavement, and the intense pain of losing someone we love, Jesus is there with us. Just as he had compassion on the widow, and his heart went out to her, so he has compassion on all who experience bereavement. In some ways this could be seen as a picture of the Resurrection, when the Bible tells us 'For as in Adam all die, so in Christ all will be made alive. But each in his own turn: Christ, the first fruits; then, when he comes, those who belong to him.' (I Cor. 15:22–23). Whenever a person experiences loss, inevitably there is a desire to replace the huge gap that is left. It is often most appropriate just to be alongside someone at times like this, as Jesus was. However, there may also be the opportunity of pointing out that just as Jesus brought back Jairus's daughter and the son of the widow at Nain, so one day he will restore to us those who have gone to be with him. If you know women who have relatives and friends who have died and who were not believers, then it is important not to comfort them with vague words of being reunited, when this may not be the case. Rather, what they need even more is the presence of Jesus with them in the midst of their grief to comfort and inspire faith.

Women as Lovers

While there are many women who go from one relationship
to the next searching for security, there are many others
with transformed or renewed hearts who, in the truest
sense, are great lovers. The woman who anointed Jesus' feet
was such a woman. In Luke 7 verses 46–50 we read of her
encounter with Jesus. Ironically, this happened in the home
of Simon, one of the Pharisees, who had invited Jesus to
dinner. Perhaps Simon had wanted to question Jesus and try
to trick him into some theological corner under the guise of
exercising hospitality. Whatever the situation, Jesus had re-
clined at the table when we are told 'a woman who had lived
a sinful life' (that is, a prostitute) entered the Pharisee's
house, knowing that Jesus was there. She must have heard of
him, maybe even seen him and experienced for herself that
there was something different about this man in comparison
with all the other men with whom she had been so intimate.
Her experience of Jesus was personal and profound. We are
told that she stood behind him at his feet, weeping, wetting
his feet with her tears. This was probably even more shock-
ing then than it would be now. Imagine a prostitute entering
a monastery or religious order, knowing that Jesus was
there! Her gestures were lavish and uncompromising. She
wiped his feet with her hair, kissed them and poured perfume upon them. Nothing could be more public and intimate yet without shame or embarrassment—at least on her
side. Her devotion was total; Simon, however, was indig-
nant, saying if Jesus were a prophet, he would know only
too well who was touching him and what kind of woman
this woman was! Jesus addressed the Pharisee by name.
'Simon,' he said, 'I have something to tell you.' In no way
was Jesus overcome, as many men may have been, by Mary's
lavish expressions of love. Rather, he told a story, the kind
the Pharisee would understand, about two men who owed
money to a certain moneylender. One owed him 500
denarii and the other 50. Neither had the money to pay him

back, so he cancelled the debts of both. Jesus asked Simon the Pharisee, 'Now which of them will love him more?' Simon replied, 'I suppose the one who had the bigger debt cancelled.' Jesus answered, 'You have judged correctly.' He then turned towards the woman and said to Simon, 'Do you see this woman? I came into your house. You did not give me any water for my feet, but she wet my feet with her tears and wiped them with her hair. You did not give me a kiss, but this woman, from the time I entered, has not stopped kissing my feet.' Jesus continued, 'You did not put oil on my head, but she has poured perfume on my feet. Therefore, I tell you, her many sins have been forgiven—for she loved much. But he who has been forgiven little loves little.' Jesus then turned to the woman and said to her, 'Your sins are forgiven . . . Your faith has saved you; go in peace.'

It is often women with great hearts—like Mary—who have given themselves lavishly and lovingly in relationships with men, who would be most open to Jesus if only they were confronted by him. It is easy to be frightened of women who stand on street corners, and to be judgemental of those we know who are caught up in endless affairs. However, among them may be some of the women most capable of loving, who once they find Jesus can turn their love outwards and lavish it upon the lonely and unloved in the world. Many women have a tremendous capacity to love and care for others. This is not always allowed full expression within our churches, nor in society at large, where professional training bars those who are uneducated from the 'caring' professions. In the West, too, we are easily embarrassed at any outward display of love and passion. We get used to physical expressions of love between men and women on TV, but not to spiritual and pastoral expressions of love in our churches and among God's people—all the more the pity. Byron, the English poet, said that 'Man's love is of man's life a thing apart, Tis a woman's whole existence.' There may be those who disagree, but it remains a fact that there are many women whose capacity to love has never

truly been awakened; and where it has, few find adequate
outlets through which to channel their passion in ways that
are truly life-giving. Women who have big hearts yet who
have never encountered Jesus need to be drawn gently to sit
at his feet and lavish their love upon him like the sinful
woman in the gospel story. Through worshipping him, our
love and passion for others is awakened and rekindled, and
there is no saying what God can do through a woman whose
heart is fully committed to him. We all know the stories of
Gladys Aylward and Mary Slessor, Mother Theresa and
Jackie Pullinger. There are many others, too, whose lives are
devoted to the 'have-nots' and the hopeless of our society,
pouring out Christ's love through their lives.

A few months ago, I was asked to represent my church at a
meeting in the civic offices, with the Mayor and a group of
people who wished to support a work initiated by an
elderly woman who lived in town. After the death of her
husband she decided to go to India for a while to recover.
While she was there her heart went out to the street
children in Bangalore. These children—tired, hungry, uncared for and parentless—strive to survive in a never-ending
struggle. They rummage in the city's litter piles for paper,
rags, discarded scraps—anything that they can sell to keep
themselves alive. Disease eats into their malnourished
bodies: bronchitis, arthritis, scabies, polio, TB and conjunc-
tivitis. Some are tempted into crime—a quick means of
solace in a life void of meaning. This woman, Liz Nunn,
nevertheless saw in them a dignity and beauty that inspired
her to help them. Liz is a woman who could so easily have
stayed at home and mourned for years over the loss of her
husband, expecting others to visit her. Instead, she went out
to others with a large heart, to bring hope and love to those
who suffered most and have least to hope for. Liz Nunn
called them the lotus children, for, she said, the lotus flower
has its roots in the mud of the bed of the lake, yet reaches up
to blossom in the light. The lotus children bed down on the
dirt of the pavement, but they too, she is convinced, can

blossom in the light—given the chance.

Liz Nunn is a challenge to every woman, especially perhaps to those who in their own loss and loneliness can reach out to others and find within themselves a largeness of heart which they never realised.

Women—Strategic in History

Although so often our history books fail to tell stories of women's presence and achievements, it is clear from the gospel accounts that women were strategic at key points in the life, death and resurrection of Jesus. It is so easy to forget that it was also a woman who, last at the cross and first at the tomb, first gave voice to the meaning of the promised Messiah. The story of the meeting of Mary and Elizabeth is a story of intimate fellowship between two women; although their mission was unique, this fellowship is repeated between women in many churches today. Elizabeth recognised the work of God's Spirit in Mary's pregnancy and in so doing said, 'Blessed is she who has believed that what the Lord has said to her will be accomplished.' Here Mary's belief is contrasted in the first chapter of Luke with Zechariah's disbelief.

Let us not be discouraged, therefore, by all the controversies that rage within the official ranks of the Church about womens' roles. Rather, we must continue to meet, women with women, to pray and share together what God is doing in our midst. The words that Mary spoke in the Magnificat could be called the first sermon witnessing to the meaning of the One who is to come. The Magnificat is undoubtedly one of the most beautiful songs of praise ever uttered. How many of us can say, as Mary said,

> My soul glorifies the Lord
>   and my spirit rejoices in God my Saviour,
> for he has been mindful
>   of the humble state of his servant.
> From now on all generations will call me blessed,

For the Mighty One has done great things for me—
holy is his name.
His mercy extends to those who fear him,
from generation to generation.
He has performed mighty deeds with his arm;
he has scattered those who are proud in their inmost
thoughts.
He has brought down rulers from their thrones
but has lifted up the humble.
He has filled the hungry with good things
but has sent the rich away empty.
He has helped his servant Israel,
remembering to be merciful
to Abraham and his descendants for ever,
even as he said to our fathers.

Obviously Mary's song had particular significance since she spoke as an Israelite within her own culture. She could not have travelled far, nor was she very learned; she did however have an understanding of the ways of the Lord that gave her a vision of a much wider world and of the scheme of things.

Pregnant Women

Pregnant women and young mothers often complain about limited horizons, especially in societies where they are thrown together while others are at work, and the only conversation seems to centre on babies and nappies and visits to the clinic. However, it is in times like these, as we shall see in this part of the book, that women can be encouraged to get together and pray together for local, national and international events—to broaden their own horizons; develop their relationship with God; and play a strategic part in the broader scheme of things as they meet and encourage each other whenever they can, in fellowship and prayer.

Throughout the gospels, women both receive and witness to Jesus' ministry of healing, teaching and preaching. In the Early Church, there was no aspect of his ministry which was kept from women. Lydia, the first convert in Europe, was a woman, and her home was used for church meetings. Priscilla and Aquilla taught believers together, again using their home as a meeting place. The traditions of the Early Church were handed on by women and men who witnessed naturally to Jesus' words and deeds.

For those who think Christianity is dull and boring, many can testify that nothing is further from the truth! Jesus delighted in taking people by surprise and doing the most unexpected things. All his actions were life-giving, breaking through sterile demands of the Law and hypocrisy. For women who are ambitious and gifted, yet who feel frustrated and stifled at home or at work, we can point out that Jesus is the One who gives us power and access into areas of life that are often naturally barred to women. In the courts of his time, for example, women were not allowed to testify, even on their own behalf. It was all the more significant, therefore, that Mary was the first witness of the Resurrection, running to the disciples and telling them that Jesus had risen! In God's providence, this was obviously not accidental. Even the first-century historian Josephus expressed a prevailing view: 'Let not the testimony of women be admitted because of the levity and boldness of their sex.' Nevertheless the Early Church's claim to Resurrection included the testimony of women because it was only women disciples, as we have seen, who were present at all the events surrounding his death. Women such as Mary and Joanna witnessed his crucifixion and death. (Luke 23:49) These same women saw the tomb and how his body was laid. (Luke 23:55) 'They found the stone rolled away from the tomb, but when they entered, they did not find the body of the Lord Jesus. While they were wondering about this, suddenly two men in clothes that gleamed like lightning stood beside them.' (Luke 24:2–4)

These women were told at the empty tomb to remember Jesus' teaching about how he must be crucified, die and rise again. Apparently they did remember, even though when they ran to tell the male disciples what they had seen and heard, the men (as is still sadly so often the case) dismissed their testimony as 'like nonsense'. (Luke 24:11)

For those who still feel that the Church is primarily a male institution, it is all the more important to introduce them to the gospels, for these clearly show from first to last that God's intention has been both seen and interpreted by women.

Kathy Keay

Kathy Keay has long been involved in evangelism—as a member of the Logos team, as a travelling secretary for the UCCF, as communications secretary at the Evangelical Alliance, and as co-ordinator of the Men, Women and God Trust in London. At college she studied English, Art and Education. Over the years she has established and still maintains many cross-cultural friendships. Now an editor with Lion Publishing, and an associate member of the Iona Community, she enjoys the arts and world travel.

3. Mothers and Toddlers

Being a mother can be exciting, exhilarating and exhausting! Nothing really prepares us for it—except practice. It is fraught with successes and failures. Our consumer society likes to depict a mother in a gleaming white kitchen, no dust, no dirt, and very little grime. The mother is dressed in an immaculate, crease-free outfit, with no sticky finger marks and no baby's dribble marks on her shoulder pads!

The toddlers in this picture are contented and good; the babies gurgle and coo. This picture of perfect motherhood pours into our homes every day through the television, press and media. It can be soul-destroying to the mother who is sitting in her living room surrounded by toys, a teething baby and a demanding toddler. It's hardly surprising that by comparison she begins to feel a failure—tired and unattractive. The continual pressure to be a stereotype of perfect motherhood defeats her.

In reality, she needs to be reassured of the good things she is doing, and that mothering is very much an individual thing. The relationship between a mother and her child is unique, and the parenting pattern for that child comes usually from the mother-child relationship. Bringing up children is hard work, because each child needs to be treated in an individual way. Children under five are usually very dependent on their mother. This increases the pressure on her. We tend to judge ourselves on how well we manage in the home, feeding, washing, ironing, dusting, and cleaning. There are times when it is very hard to keep up with these duties, especially for women who have been brought up to believe that they are entirely a woman's responsibility. As mothers we must realise that this is not a reflection on our failure to cope with the family. Sometimes we feel the priority must be a tidy house and meals on time, ironing up to date. In striving for this we can miss out on important times of sharing experiences and exploring things together with our children. As an older mother now, when I visit families the young mother will always say 'excuse the mess'. For me, these scenes are filled with tired but happy memories of when my children were this age, and I sometimes long for them again.

Expectations and Realities of Motherhood

Every woman from the earliest years of her life is conditioned to believe that one day she will become a wife, then a mother. Such pressure can be very hard on those who do not marry, want to develop their career, find it difficult to conceive a child, or when they have children want to return to work. Women in these situations have felt isolated, and it is only in the last few years that society has begun to be aware of their dilemma. The Church needs to follow suit.

For most couples the conception of a child is a cause for celebration. As the pregnancy progresses the expectations of motherhood are very high. The mother may work until she is 28 weeks pregnant or more, and many decide to take maternity leave from work, fully intending to return to work after the birth. She will spend the last few weeks before the birth preparing herself at home, making everything ready for the baby's arrival. Medically, she will be prepared; she will have been carefully monitored before the birth, she may have decided how she will have the baby, and feel she is ready for the change the baby will bring.

When the baby is born, she begins to realise that motherhood is an endless round of feeding and changing, trying to work everything else around the baby. She may be thrilled with her baby, but she didn't expect to feel so tired. Shopping with a baby is a difficult experience; trying to cross the road pushing her precious bundle in front of her can reduce her to a hopeless wreck.

Those early months of looking after the first baby contain a lot of worrying and hoping she's done the right thing. I remember I used to look at my baby and the nappies which I could never put on the same way twice, and wonder if the poor thing would ever manage to walk properly! She did, and all that worry was unnecessary. The first time the baby does anything new becomes a landmark: the first smile, the first inoculation, the first tooth, the first word, the first step —and suddenly that baby is a toddler. It's then that a mother may begin to realise that she has lost confidence in herself, and feels unsure about what she should do next. At this stage she may conceive another baby, and find herself with a baby and a toddler. The learning process of the first baby makes it easier as everyone feels more experienced with the bathing and nappy changing. The new difficulty lies in helping the toddler accept the new arrival. In a sensitive and loving way the mother will help the child overcome feelings of jealousy.

When we review the first few years of motherhood, none of us is exempt from the joys and heartache, the excitement as we watch the children grow, the exhaustion as they exert their wills! As Christians we experience all these things and more. More—because through all the hardships, we have the Lord Jesus to help and direct us. When we have a living faith in him, He fills us each day with his love and peace as we confess our sin and guilt to him. (1 John 1:9) Christian mothers feel tense, emotional and vulnerable just like other women. We can turn to Jesus and ask Him to come into our lives in a fresh way, and he does. We also get lonely, isolated and need friendships. There come times in every young mother's experience when she feels isolated and lonely and wants more contact than just in her home, with her husband and children. This can be a deep need, especially for the woman who has moved away from the area where she was brought up. It is on this basis that in recent years many churches have become aware of the needs of young mothers and their children and have started Mother and Toddler groups. This can be a valuable means of reaching young families in the community.

Mother and Toddler Groups

'All over the British Isles mothers and young children are meeting in what are known as Mother and Toddler clubs. Women expecting babies, fathers, grandparents, child minders and anyone interested in helping are usually welcome as well.' So writes Joyce Donogue in *Running a Toddler Club.*

Mother and Toddler groups can become an important part of a young mother's life. In the group she can talk to other mothers, share ideas, and her children can meet others and play. It's a place where she can see that her children are similar to others, that they demand and cry for basically the same things. Mothers can laugh together at their toddlers' latest antics, when bath essence is poured down the toilet, and lipstick is used to make a nice picture on Mummy's bedroom wall!

The initial visit to the group can be difficult for the mother because it may be some time since she has made contact with other adults outside her immediate circle. It is hard to walk into a room of strange women and their children. Some weeks ago when I was visiting a group, I watched a new mother walk up and down outside several times before plucking up courage to come in. Sometimes they don't make it. She later shared with me that she nearly went home again, but one of the other mothers came up to her and said 'Hello', and this broke the ice. It is important if we attend or lead a group to make sure that newcomers are made to feel welcome.

These groups are usually held in a large hall, a room in a church or community centre, and sometimes in homes. The format of each group may vary, but usually there is tea or coffee for the mothers and drinks for children. Large toys are at hand such as toddler trikes, buses, and cars to ride in. There are push and pull prams, trolleys and trains. Some groups may have climbing blocks, frames and slides.

In the life of a toddler, everything is a voyage of discovery, from smelling a flower, flooding the bathroom, watching insects, to throwing a tantrum. To increase the child's awareness, the group will provide activities to encourage the child's basic manipulative skills: painting, playdough, sticking, drawing, jigsaws and puzzles, sand and water play. These groups are usually noisy, hectic, harrowing but rewarding. The Pre-school Playgroups Association has representatives who will come and advise anyone who would like to start a toddler group. This is an excellent secular organisation that has worked alongside many churches to help them set up toddler groups and playgroups. Other ideas for activities and helping mums in a group can be obtained from the CPAS ministry to young mothers.

As Christian mothers reach out into the community, we can be praying that God will use the group to bring young families to know Jesus. There are times when mothers in the group are going through difficult times. Their child may be going through tantrums, or being destructive, and they may feel overwhelmed. They may not feel they can cope very well with the pressures of motherhood and may be depressed. As Christians we need to give them the chance to share, making them feel accepted and that we value them. These mothers need our love, our time and our friendship. Some groups run a crisis line for practical help; women from the church will visit and help with housework and shopping.

There may be times in the context of the group when a

mum may experience difficulties and there may be the opportunity to pray. At one group a crawling baby knocked over a mug of hot coffee. The baby was taken to the cold water tap; a cold compress was applied to the arm. The leader prayed for the baby and the distraught mother. No scald resulted! The Lord answers prayer, though not always so dramatically. The mum was amazed. This incident gave the Christians in the group a good opportunity to share their faith. Likewise as we trust the Lord he will give us the opportunities to share the Good News. We can celebrate the victory of a child who has overcome a fear or a speech defect. Such opportunities usually come as a result of friendship and sharing God's love in everyday situations.

In visiting toddler groups used as community outreach in and around the London area, I have come to the following conclusions.

1. There are significant numbers of mothers from the community attending these groups.

2. Often not enough Christian mothers carry the practical burdens for running these. More church back-up is necessary, perhaps using older women to help.

3. Some Christian women are nervous about making friends and sharing their faith. They need teaching in introducing friendship evangelism, and encouragement from their church in what they are doing.

4. Many groups run special outreach suppers and coffee mornings, and use Christmas and Easter to have special services in their churches.

5. Many groups use the resources in the local community e.g. library, health visitor, PPA rep, Early Learning materials. These are good as they make good links with the community.

Judi Richards

Judi Richards is an educational home visitor with young families in Brixton, London. She is also co-ordinator of creche workers for Lambeth Education Institute and served on the womens' committee of Mission to London in 1985. Judi is married with two daughters.

4. Self-employed Women at Home: Bumpsadaisy: the Shape of Things to Come

Out-of-the-ordinary maternity clothes are often hard to find; they are usually expensive, too. Most women cannot justify spending a lot of money on clothes that are worn for about six months of pregnancy and then discarded, and yet mothers-to-be naturally want to look and feel good, to have their morale boosted by an attractive wardrobe! When I was expecting our third child, I felt exceedingly bored, and fed up with wearing the maternity clothes that had already seen me through two pregnancies! I longed for a change—and as I enjoy clothes anyway, I was also longing for some attractive new additions to my wardrobe. But my husband was a curate, and we couldn't spend money on new maternity clothes.

I felt frustrated. Why didn't someone lend me something new? Friends kindly did, but the dresses had already done the pregnancies of the rest of the Young Wives' group, and I ungratefully felt worse than ever!

'If only I could hire something for a change,' I moaned to my long-suffering husband. He replied that maybe I should take the initiative and start the hire service myself! That took a little while to sink in—but he encouraged me to think about it, and eventually the idea of a maternity hire service was born, together with its name—'Bumpsadaisy'.

Small Beginnings

I hadn't run a business before and had very little idea how to go about it professionally. So it all started very simply. Armed with a loan and a cheque book, I set out to buy a selection of maternity clothes. I scoured the local papers and bought lots of good quality second-hand garments, as well as some new ones, and—I can add with hindsight—made several mistakes in my purchases! I then put some small adverts into the local papers and ante-natal clinics and distributed leaflets to friends and neighbours.

The night before that very first Bumpsadaisy morning, I hardly slept for worrying about what I was doing! I was convinced that no one would turn up; it was all a dreadful mistake, and curates' wives shouldn't do such things anyway! I put the clothes out that first morning, and to my amazement, two women turned up! I should have had more faith —I had gone ahead with the conviction that this scheme had the Lord behind it.

The first two weeks of business were quite good. Several garments went out on hire; I met some pleasant people, and everything seemed to be going well. Then came the morning when no one turned up at all! I very nearly gave up then and there—but my husband urged me to give it a few months before I made any rash decisions. He was right—it does take time for a new business to grow, and gradually over the next few months custom picked up and everything went very well.

Then came the time for my husband to move to a new job. By this time I had established a thriving, if very small, business. So we found a friend to take over once we had moved away from Norwich, and I started another Bumpsadaisy in Bath. This time we were living in a small village, and it took longer for business to get established. After six months I was just about to give up when a Christian magazine published an article about Bumpsadaisy, which I had sent to them some time before. The response from other young Christian mothers was amazing—they wanted to run Bumpsadaisys too in their local areas. I had to decide: should I simply tell them how to do it; or should I take the plunge and start a Bumpsadaisy franchise company? After a lot of prayer and thought we decided to go nationwide. We knew nothing about running such a scheme and had no idea how to enter the rag trade and get clothes at less than retail price. But many prayers were answered, and small but significant miracles meant that three months later we had seven branches waiting to start!

We went into one shop and dared to ask if I could have a discount if I bought their maternity dungarees in bulk! The shop assistant was slightly taken aback and called the manageress. My husband explained what we were doing and to our amazement (what little faith!) she gave us a back copy of the relevant trade magazine and explained how one orders stock from suppliers and their agents. I telephoned the two nearest agents, who came with their samples—and both let us order new stock and buy samples at 40% off wholesale price as it was the end of the season! This was an unexpected bonus which greatly helped us for several seasons.

Learning Lessons

I began to learn about forward ordering, advertising copy, accounts and computing. I had to write a Training Manual for the new branches—and managed to 'lose' most of it on the computer the first time, and had to start again! With three small children and a husband who was a school chaplain, plus my own part-time teaching in the school, and the school Bible studies which met at our home in the evenings, I began to feel slightly harrassed! At the same time, my father died after a year of heart trouble, and various other members of both our families were ill. It was not an easy period for us. One of the things we had to learn was to 'receive' from our friends. We knew that it is more blessed to give than to receive and it was difficult for us to receive help from our friends. They were marvellous, nevertheless, helping with their prayers and time, by being available and showing concern.

By September 1984 the first seven branches of Bumpsadaisy were ready to open—and I spent several nights packing up parcels into the small hours in order to get the stock off to them. The autumn term began, and my son Robin, aged five and a half, went off to school. Harriet, three, started to go each morning; that left Victoria, aged eighteen months, still at home. Then came another answer to prayer. Heather, a young Christian friend who had spent a few weeks with us over the summer, decided to stay for a year as our nanny. It was a relief to know that the children would be looked after by someone I could trust. She also did the housework and ironing, while I took over the children from tea-time. I felt that it was important to be there after school, and at bedtime; and the children adored Heather and had great fun with her during the day. They benefited from a slightly less busy mother, and from parents who had more time together. With Heather living in we could sometimes go out in the evenings without too much difficulty, and we have found that to be important.

Bumpsadaisy began to go from strength to strength. National advertising in relevant magazines brought us a large post and enquiries from other people wanting to start branches. We began to expand, but it was often hard work and worrying whether we would be able to meet deadlines, especially when the bills began to come in. One thing I have had to learn several times is to 'tithe' my income. It has often been quite difficult to give away hard-earned and much needed income, but whenever I have organised myself and begun to do it regularly, my income has gone up. It is extraordinary; it has happened with the business account to a certain extent, but has been most noticeable with my local Bumpsadaisy. 'God is no one's debtor,' my mother frequently tells me, and she's right; he is gracious enough to be interested in Bumpsadaisy!

Eighteen months after our move to Bath, my husband was asked to consider coming to London to a large central church. I was heart-broken! Life was just beginning to settle down; the children were happily settled at school, and the business seemed to be going fairly well, both with the nationwide set-up and with customers once more coming locally to hire. I spent six miserable months dreading the move, and worrying that the substantial drop in salary would prove to be very difficult. We had a dear friend who was an evangelist staying with us at one time, preaching in the school chapel. He said he would pray that Bumpsadaisy would make up the difference, once we had moved. Naturally, I was sceptical, but also curious, because Jim's prayers are usually 'powerful and effective'. (James 5:16) My husband knew that the Lord was calling him to London, and this was confirmed by the attitude of colleagues. He also felt sure that I would enjoy it once we were there!

The Move to London

So after just two years in Bath, we came to London. The church found us a large house, big enough to give me my own study/showroom for the business, but sadly without a garden, so we left our dog with friends in Bath! Bumpsadaisy now had thirty branches and a London address and telephone number in adverts. That seemed to make a big difference right from the start. It somehow gave credibility to the business; ours had been a Limpley Stoke exchange, which doesn't somehow have the same ring about it! Our suppliers and advertising places are now nearly all within easy reach, which has been an enormous help. So there were immediate advantages to moving.

The children all began new schools as soon as we had moved, all three now going full time. I was able to work nearly all day—and most evenings as well, often just to answer the post and send out all the brochures. With no help in the house, with business increasing, and being ill myself, I resented London. I missed the wide open spaces and beautiful rolling hills of the Cotswolds, the ease of baby-sitters from the school sixth form, the small friendly church family I had left.

I needed help desperately, so I put a small advert in the local newsagent's window, and prayed hard that I'd find a reliable cleaning lady! I had two almost immediately—Jo, recently graduated in Classics and unable to find a job, who began by cleaning the house but was soon established as a part-time secretary; and Virginia, with several degrees in Fine Arts, and trying to pay her way as an artist, willing to clean in order to pay for her studio. *Thank you, Lord.*

Bumpsadaisy began to grow again— up to forty branches open now, but sadly we had lost some along the way. Three dropped out because it simply hadn't worked for them. I felt guilty—had I not helped them enough? Were they in the wrong area? Other people assured me that some small businesses just don't work, sometimes because people are simply not suited to the job; but I still feel personally involved and guilty if things don't go well for a branch. On the other hand, it has been lovely to hear from the Christian women involved, who write and tell me how they've prayed when things haven't gone well, and how the Lord has answered their prayers with increased business. Lesley in Glasgow said, 'Every Monday night I pray that the Lord will take Bumpsadaisy and use it for Him. I trust Him to meet my financial needs, and He does just that.'

Christian Hospitality

During our first year in London the prayers of our evangelist friend began to be answered by my local Bumpsadaisy hire. (Despite working almost full time on the nationwide company, I was still running and still do run a local branch, which is what I enjoy best.) My local customers were hiring special occasion and evening wear—lovely clothes from abroad that I enjoy working with. It meant that the local takings were soon sufficient to begin to help pay bills and school fees. Meeting people is always interesting; but when they are young mothers-to-be it is especially rewarding. Those of us who run Bumpsadaisys and are Christians, find that we meet many women we wouldn't otherwise see. Some are in need of help, others are very open to the Gospel. It's very easy to talk to customers in a natural way about the new baby or the rest of the family. Often we get to know our customers fairly well if they come back to hire over several months. On one occasion I asked a customer if she was expecting her first baby, and she hesitated, saying 'Yes', then 'Well, no—yes in a way.' She went on to explain that she had lost her first baby in a cot death not long before. She was naturally still very upset about it, and we had a long talk. Another customer sat down with a cup of coffee before trying things on, and we started chatting. She was expecting twins after 13 miscarriages, and the doctor warned that this pregnancy was in danger too. Naturally, she was very upset, and we talked. Soon after, she was admitted to hospital for complete rest, but did sadly miscarry once more, and I didn't see her again.

I often feel an urgency about talking to these mothers-to-be. People are usually very open to discussing 'religion' when thinking about the miracle of conception and birth; and many are in need of support when going through the traumas of bringing up small children. Yet they are customers for Bumpsadaisy, as well as being in my home, and it is necessary to be courteous and not pushy or over-enthusiastic! To speak a 'word in season' doesn't normally come naturally to me, and it is often necessary to learn when to speak and when to be silent! It may be right to invite customers along to a Young Wives' group at church; sometimes a cup of coffee and a sympathetic ear are sufficient. Certainly my local customers have no idea that I'm a clergy-man's wife. I think that's a good thing, as I don't like being labelled and find it easier to talk to them if they don't know, at least to begin with. Some customers are obviously not wanting to make it a 'social' visit in any case. Most are extremely friendly and nice to meet and come to hire a dress; they don't stop for coffee! When I first started Bumpsadaisy, my open morning became a glorified coffee morning, and was advertised as such with tea and coffee always available; customers used to sit and chat, and enjoyed seeing people again on return visits. Some Bumpsadaisy branches still operate like this; I have become more formal from necessity. With a secretary also working in the room, and constant office phone calls, my showroom is less easy to sit in and socialise than the sitting-room used to be. In a way that's sad as the customer contact remains a potentially important evangelistic opportunity.

The Joys and Trials of Working at Home

Working from home has tremendous advantages with a young family. For instance, the day that Harriet cut her forehead at school, I was able to go immediately. I can pop downstairs mid-morning when the washing machine has finished and hang up the clothes. Everything is always to hand, and I'm available whenever needed, by husband or children.

Having the office at home also keeps overheads down, as things like the telephone, computer and photocopier can be used for business and home. And it's easy to finish a job in the evenings after the children have gone to bed, without the need of babysitters. My children are still young enough to go to bed early, which gives me another two or three hours to work most evenings, when my husband is out at church. Our fellowship group meets once a fortnight, but otherwise I appreciate those few hours to catch up on work without too many interruptions (and often begrudge having to stop to do the ironing!)

However, there are tremendous disadvantages, too. There is a temptation both ways—either not to work when one should, or to work when one should be with the family. I'm at my desk by nine am each weekday, after an hour's round trip to school. Breakfast is a very hurried affair—while the children eat theirs, I'm usually emptying the dishwasher from the night before, or doing last-minute packed lunches. We're out of the house at eight o'clock, and it's always a rush! My continual resolution is to go to bed earlier in order to get up earlier so that I can spend time in Bible study and then get the children dressed (they are still small enough to need help) and fed in a leisurely manner. I'm left wondering how the 'Wife of noble character' in Proverbs 31 managed it all. 'She gets up while it is still dark; she provides food for her family ... and her lamp does not go out at night' (Prov. 31:15,18).

In theory the daily early hour of Bible study developed in student days should grow into a lasting habit. Yet I have found this almost impossible with tiny babies, when nights are disturbed and the baby's cries interrupt me as soon as I sit down. I have learnt instead to take a verse—often a well-loved one—and meditate on it while doing the ironing, washing up or feeding the baby. With busy days now to make a new business work, and a young family to care for, this habit has continued in its shortened form: a walk to the post office, a journey, a few quiet minutes after the children have gone to bed before I return to my desk. Certainly the early morning is no longer a suitable time.

From nine o'clock onwards my day is spent in the office/showroom—a lovely large room, where Jo and I work, customers browse and the telephone hardly ever stops ringing!

It seems important that Christian principles be rigorously applied in business. It would sometimes be all too easy to get angry with customers or telephone callers, or even to fiddle the books. Instead, I need to use quick 'arrow' prayers for help, and all too often forget! I'm very conscious of the fact that many of the franchisees know I'm a clergyman's wife; with the Christians there is a wonderful sense of fellowship right from the start, but with the others I am conscious of the need to bend over backwards to be fair and do the best I can. On the other hand, it's such a relief to be able to pray about the business, usually with my husband, and to bring our needs and requests to God. Often we need to learn to do that first, rather than as a last resort!

Working at home means that friends often think that 'my hobby' must be amusing, but don't seem to realise that it is full-time! It's difficult if people drop in unexpectedly during the day for coffee, and hard not to be unwelcoming, spending the time worrying about the work which isn't being done upstairs! I'm expected to be able to help with school activities or Young Wives' groups in a way that wouldn't be assumed at all if I actually went out to an office each day. I have to be firm, risking offence, when explaining the situation. I feel that it isn't right to try to do everything (despite the example of the proverbial woman!) Past experience of doing too much shows that it is always the family who suffer. If I'm tired, or under pressure, or just extra busy, then I don't spend enough time with them, and I become irritable. Pressure can lead to resentment, too—wanting to get on with exciting new business ideas, yet having to stop to collect the children from school or to cook a meal. It's no fun for them if Mummy or Daddy is always too busy to take the bikes out or to go swimming. It means making an extra special effort at weekends, for instance, to be with them and do something together. At the back of my mind, too, is the thought that it won't be too long before they are grown and no longer wanting us around anyway! The best time each day is the time I spend alone with each one at bedtime. 'Lights out' is staggered to give each about a quarter of an hour with me; I enjoy it and I hope that they do! We talk, read a bedtime story, and say prayers together. I help Robin with his *Quest* notes—appreciating the simple thought myself, and yet feeling privileged to help him with his daily Bible reading. Robin asked Jesus into his heart in the middle of church one Sunday morning after singing 'if you want joy, real joy, ask Jesus to come into your heart'. Harriet knelt by her bed one evening with me and shyly asked Jesus to become real to her, too. Moments like these are incomparable and important—more so than any business deals!

Sometimes I need to be reminded of that. The business can become all-pervading, either with exciting new ideas or with worries and doubts. Many nights we've not slept because the business was occupying our minds. And there have been occasions when I've not concentrated on my husband or children because I was preoccupied with business. I enjoy Bumpsadaisy very much; but there is Jesus' warning to remember: 'No-one can serve two masters. Either he will hate the one and love the other, or he will be devoted to the one and despise the other. You cannot serve both God and Money.' (Matt. 6:24) For a woman to succeed in business these days is perfectly feasible; but it must not be at the expense either of her Christian life or of her family life. 'A woman who fears the Lord is to be praised. Give her the reward she has earned, and let her works bring her praise at the city gate.' (Prov. 31:30–31)

Penny Swithinbank

Penny Swithinbank is founder and co-ordinator of Bumpsadaisy, a franchise which promotes maternity clothes throughout the UK. A trained secondary school teacher, she is married to Kim and mother of three children. They are currently based at All Souls Langham Place, where Kim is Director of Evangelism.

5. Involvement for the Full-time Housewife

If contentment could be pictured within family life in a provincial city, then Sally and John provided a good illustration. For the two of them, a life of marital domesticity really worked. Both were satisfied with their lives. John's job was going well. The children enjoyed home and friends. Sally was creating an environment for a happy family. Everything in the garden seemed rosy. Something was bound to go wrong sooner or later, but it didn't. Contrary to so many popular Christian testimonies, Sally and John didn't face demoralisation, desperation or death in order to acknowledge their need for Jesus Christ—all they did was go to a disco!

Involvement in the Parent Teachers' Association brings together Christians and non-Christians within the local community. In this case, the chairman was a Christian, who was faced with the last-minute problem of getting a disc-jockey booked for the PTA annual fund-raising disco. What he did was to draft a Christian friend, who was also a semi-professional disc-jockey.

This man travelled over a hundred miles to lead the disco. Christians attended from the local church without compromising either their faith or conduct. A bridge of friendship was built, but without any direct testimony to Jesus. However, the atmosphere, the absence of smutty stories and dirty jokes all told their own story. The disco was highly successful and raised a great deal of money.

Soon Sally and John were in church, and within a year had committed their lives to Jesus Christ.

Why do I tell this story? The names are fictitious, but the event happened. It is easy to conduct evangelism in big meetings within a Christian context where we feel comfortable. Going into the community and learning how to be Christian without compromise is however another matter. 'Holiness' learnt by withdrawing from society is far simpler than developing holy lives within the world in which we live. Developing relationships within our local community, getting alongside neighbours and colleagues, allowing our words and lives to speak for Jesus, all these present the most radical, costly yet necessary challenge for Christians anywhere today.

How far should we be involved? Should Christians go to discos? Can we be involved in non-Christian associations? These are not easy questions, but they are certainly relevant. While this involvement has been right for me, every Christian woman must follow her conscience on these matters—at the same time allowing the consciences of others to disagree!

Women at Work

For centuries, the Church has been consciously or subconsciously suppressing the rights of women to fulfil a major role within the body of Christ. Generally it is the men who speak, the men who evangelise, the men who make decisions, the men who pray. This can be discouraging for women to the point that we can be tempted to opt out of any sense of responsibility for ministry at all. Some women become passive, stay at home, semi-hermits, while others rise up in indignation and try to change the system.

God has made each of us differently. We have a unique capacity to respond to his love, surrender our lives to him and receive his commission to reach our particular part of the world for him. Each of us can begin where we are.

Opportunities to engage in acts of kindness, to open our homes to others, to take on a role within the community are there for each of us to engage in as we respond to God's individual direction in our lives. Whether in a family or alone, young or old, female or male, we all possess the gift and calling of God in our lives. Our duty is to recognise and obey it!

Rather than putting ourselves down and believing that God can use only men, we in fact have much to teach men when it comes to gossiping the Gospel in casual conversation. Women are often more natural, spontaneous and open in sharing their faith.

Prayer and evangelism go hand in hand. The development of groups like the Lydia Fellowship have in recent years helped to mobilise enormous initiatives in evangelism among women.

Making the most of schemes like Prayer Triplets (instituted during Mission England and Mission to London) or taking up the responsibility for being a Light in Every Street ('LES') these simple schemes can be used to encourage women to get together in groups of three or four pledging to pray each week.[1] From our praying, mutual encouragement and support often emerge so that we are able to witness more effectively to our non-Christian friends and neighbours.

Women to Women

Increasingly I have been developing a concern for different women, all represented within the local church family. Women who are married to non-Christians, or to church leaders, or who are separated or divorced—all these are fortunate if they ever get out at night! If evenings are difficult times to meet, then daytime activities can be encouraged for women who don't go out to work.

In our area, we have divided women into small prayer cells where they can support and pray for each other. On a monthly basis we all meet together for general teaching sessions. Many churches are beginning to think in similar ways. Cell groups, evangelistic and non-evangelistic, aerobic classes, study groups and evangelistic lunches can all play their part. Our local Italian restaurant has already offered the use of its facilities to put on an evangelistic lunch.

Study sessions taking an in-depth look at current issues such as the role of women, unemployment, or the bomb provide other possible meeting points. Paul encouraged us by saying 'I have become all things to all men so that by all possible means I might save some.' (I Cor. 9:22)

The Church needs to accept its God-given role to be salt and light. Paul Tournier indicated in his book *The Gift of Feeling* that women can play a vital part. A woman's sensitivity to the moods and needs of others can be a major asset in counselling. Whether it is at the tennis club or the local leisure centre, the world goes on often without Christian influence. It is time that we women as well as men got our hands dirty and became more fully involved.

The Challenge

The announcement of a church visitation programme often fills many of us with horror. We prefer to visit homes on the opposite side of the estate, yet it is our neighbours and friends with whom we have the greatest contact and who can become most open to the Gospel. It is not surprising that many of us suffer a real loss of nerve! I know that my life should be totally open to God, that I should be prepared to 'gossip the Gospel' to my friends, but I find it far easier to share Jesus with strangers than with neighbours.

All ABCs of evangelism and neat theological formulae become redundant when we are talking naturally to a friend. We need to learn to express truth with integrity and sincerity, and not just through well-practised phrases learnt off by heart. At the same time it is important to remember that when the truth is rejected even by the nicest and most caring friends, this condemns them to an eternity without God. Telling them these things can easily challenge our friendship, but if we really care for people it will be a challenge worth taking. Over the years, I have had to learn a loving, caring, forthright but careful approach towards my friends and neighbours. Sometimes I'm still afraid and miss many opportunities, but I am committed to the fact that our Christianity must work practically in our everyday lives and not just become the subject of our preaching.

Whoever we are, we probably relate best to people with lives similar to our own. As a mother with four children, I tend to be at my most relaxed in the company of other young mothers. The pressures and joys of children, homes and husbands provide us with much in common. Our priorities differ, but the problems of life are similar for Christians and non-Christians alike. Conversation with women like myself provides a host of opportunities to speak honestly about Jesus.

Housewives Are Not Gullible

We live in a high-powered, supergloss consumer society, where the media, TV and door-to-door salesmen pump their own individual message home.

'This powder washes whiter'—'Or was it that one?'
'Why doesn't this polish cut my cleaning time in half?'

It is little wonder that many housewives are automatically suspicious of slick, professional salesmen who claim to have found the right solution to everyday domestic problems. Easy answers are quickly rejected. In fact instead of being the most gullible of people as is sometimes thought, house-wives who have become wise in spotting Jehovah's Witnesses and rejecting anything that looks cheap or too time-consuming will easily say 'no' to evangelical Christianity, if it is presented in impersonal sales language.

How To Get Started

How do we make contact with women and their families? Like every group of people, women need to be understood. Being a wife and mother who chooses not to take up professional employment outside the home, I become rather weary of conversations which run, 'What do you do?'

> 'I'm a wife and mother.'
> 'Oh, you don't have a job then?'

For women in my position, this can be undermining. Some mothers are able to live full and satisfying professional lives. Others such as myself do not or cannot. Our husbands are away too often working and we view our role at home too highly to leave the children on their own. This is our choice. When meeting other women who have made these choices, it is important to build up their self-esteem and not to make them feel like second-class citizens.

However, it is important also to remember that many women who work outside the home have no choice. They are either single-parent families, divorced or single women who have no alternative source of income.

Becoming a Mother

Many women find the changes involved in becoming a mother rather dramatic! It is a far cry from working for example as a busy personal assistant facing a demanding task in an expanding company, to washing nappies in the isolation of an empty house! The shock can be equally as great shifting from working at a checkout till in the local supermarket, chatting to the customers, to finding the only conversation at home lies in a screaming, inarticulate bundle of flesh! However much a baby may have been wanted, adapting to its arrival in the home can often prove to be painful and emotionally draining. It's easy to feel mentally devalued and emotionally stressed, and the Christian mother may feel spiritually useless as well as depressed. It's here that a positive and active role in Mother and Toddler Groups, playgroups, pre-school nurseries, and other activities for younger children can form an important meeting point between young mothers of all kinds. Most young mothers these days have to go through the routine of exercise classes and ante-natal clinics, and it is here that a large mission field awaits any Christian woman who wants to make the most of her circumstances in reaching out to others.

Mothers in any culture cannot avoid rubbing shoulders. Among them will be those who may feel isolated and frustrated in their new role. Beginning some kind of support group can provide a valuable service within the local community. The church in recent years has opened its eyes to the need of providing resources and encouragement for Christians to be involved in such groups. Though the initiative still lies with the women to get something going, church leaders can be encouraged to see that when their premises are used in this way, relationships can be made which may help to bring other women to a Christian faith. Sometimes non-Christians feel more secure if their children are placed in a 'religious' setting, and Christian support groups can provide an important alternative to their non-Christian counterparts within any local community.

Most women would have to be extremely shy to survive a Mother and Toddler Group without being drawn into the conversation. The meeting often brings a sense of release from being cooped up with nappy talk at home. It is a welcome relief to talk to another adult, while the children benefit from group play.

Child Evangelists

The relationships that children develop between themselves can in turn lead parents to get to know each other. Even babies can play a part! It is amazing how people will stop in the street to admire a newborn baby. Interest and contact can be created between children and parents in a whole variety of ways. Often a pregnancy gives the opportunity for a friendly word, followed by a bunch of flowers and a card when the baby is born. Relationships between women during pregnancy, birth and aftercare can grow into lasting friendships that spread between both families. This is not surprising, as this period is usually one of the most important in a woman's life—if she has children.

Developing an Open Home

In this context our homes can take on a new significance. Too often, we protect them as our own. Yet as Christians, we have no biblical mandate to live in isolation from the wider community. This is a Western pattern which needs to be broken down. God's call on our lives is to love our neighbours and open our homes to them.

The other day I had an evening all to myself. The children were in bed and my husband was preaching away from home. For several days, I had anticipated this time to catch up with all the things which I had been putting aside. No sooner had I sat down when the telephone rang. A single parent living nearby really needed someone to talk to. At first I was annoyed, but I invited her round. For half an hour I struggled to be civil. Why had God taken away my only free night? Yet in the end the time we spent together was good for me and reassuring for her. God's ways, demands and timing are not always ours, but when we listen to him our lives become fruitful.

Our homes when opened can become places in which friendships can be formed. Other mothers and families can be invited in for coffee or lunch. Often this means that the husbands get together as well! Potluck lunches provide quick and easy solutions for people who don't want too much work on their hands. If a neighbour's children come to play while she has a quiet visit to the shops, everyone benefits. Sharing the car with others as joint transport for the weekly shopping trip can be another important way of doing things together and developing friendships. As we allow the Holy Spirit to influence the whole of our lives,

God's activity is not limited to church meetings but operates unhindered through individual lives committed utterly to him.

Gatecrashing the System

The years involved in looking after young children can provide a Christian mother with some of the best opportunities for sharing her faith. In Bible times, there was no school gate. The equivalent was the village well. Scripture records many significant meetings at the village well. Abraham's servant met Rebekah (Gen. 23); Jacob found Rachel (Gen. 29); Moses met Zipporah (Exod. 2); and Jesus instigated a life-changing encounter with the woman at Sychar. (John 4)

In the East where water was scarce, the well provided the natural meeting place for women. Today's equivalent for young mothers is the school gate. In 1982 Eddie Gibbs, the training Director of Mission England, announced that the school gate provided possibly 'the best opportunity for evangelism in Britain today'. I want to endorse this, and to emphasise that it is an opportunity limited by time. After only a few years, a mother will no longer make that daily pilgrimage.

I have learnt four lessons at the school gate:

1. Listen to non-Christian parents.
2. Don't preach, but give relevant alternatives to their own viewpoints.
3. Establish friendship as the basis for everything else.
4. Realise the importance of prayer.

At the school gate I am a missionary; I must pray and need prayer from my housegroup and local congregation.

Even the 'lollipop man' who guides the children across the main road, can become a friend who sees the Gospel as relevant to him in a way that he may never encounter if he only heard a sermon.

Apart from being friendly and ready to listen, the easiest

way of being accepted and recognised within the school community is to get involved with the local Parent Teacher Association (PTA). However busy we are, my husband and I have agreed that one of us should try to be on the committee. It is easy to become caught up in so many church commitments that an involvement of this kind is almost impossible. I've found it to be really worthwhile (though we all have to find out what is right for us).

Take for example the first six weeks of this term. For me they have involved collecting and selling jumble, cleaning out the PTA shed, making 21 soft toys (British bulldogs in the England football strip!) and helping to prepare over 200 lunches at the school fair. Getting involved in these activities has been high on my priority list, because they provide opportunities to work in direct relationship with non-Christian mums.

When Parents Pray

Mothers can extend their influence further by changing attitudes towards the classroom. When school is not simply viewed as a dumping ground for one's prodigies, but an opportunity not only for education but for playing a vital role within the community, all kinds of possibilities for involvement open up. For example, helping in classes and assisting in the teaching in a voluntary capacity where needed, opens up new relationships with teachers and pupils alike.

Two years ago, our family moved to London. As I went to and from the school gate and observed other Christian mothers, I longed to see them getting involved with the school. Consequently, I suggested that rather than standing all together waiting for our children, we could begin praying for the needs of the school, staff and parents. As a result, I was nominated to approach the headteacher and ask for her permission to do this. I must confess it wasn't easy, and I was rather fearful at this point! However, this proved to be quite unnecessary. For while she was careful to point out the need for caution and sensitivity, on the whole she was most supportive. She warned us about being too personal in our prayers and trying to score points against children who might be antagonistic towards our own sons or daughters.

With this in mind, we started constructive praying, and with the headteacher's endorsement, a monthly prayer meeting began and was soon recognised as an official function of the PTA! It is now advertised in PTA newsletters and a regular report is given to the Annual General Meeting of the PTA! We meet each month in our home, which is in walking distance of the school. Parents are all free to come, and many do so, along with at least two of the teachers. We eat a potluck lunch (each tries to bring a contribution). Some definite answers to prayer have emerged from these times, and non-Christian mothers have begun to ask if we can pray for them in times of personal crises—even if they would never dream of attending themselves.

Often these requests focus on health matters. One child had been suffering from an illness which made close contact extremely unpleasant. This continued for some years. Soon after we began praying, a diagnosis was given and the problem solved. The husband of one staff member was self-employed. He was disabled as a result of a chronic injury and had been prevented from working for more than a year. None of us knows what part prayer played in his recovery, but we do believe that it was significant that he soon recovered sufficiently to resume work. Our prayer times have also included prayer for school activities of all kinds, with encouraging results. Prayer is our lifeline to God, and I could elaborate on many incidents where we have seen God's hand at work in response to our regular, inadequate but sincere prayers.

It is not always easy to measure prayer in terms of results, but since we started praying regularly, we've noticed the following:

1. We have an increasing awareness that God is concerned about all areas of our lives.
2. Non-Christian parents gain a greater 'God-awareness.'
3. Friendships are created and strengthened as we have talked and prayed while our children fight over the toys!
4. Excellent relations have emerged with the headteacher and staff. The school has always kept a strong church link, but this initiative has created a deep sense of mutual involvement and concern between teachers and Christian parents.
5. Commitment to the school has given us other opportunities. There has been a healthy and growing sense of partnership within school affairs, which has created a climate of constructive conversation rather than the criticism or silence which is so often the case.

Ruth Calver

Note

[1]Prayer Triplets are groups of Christians, usually known to each other, who meet in threes in order to pray for friends and neighbours. The triplet scheme was initiated prior to Mission England in 1984, and through it hundreds of people were converted before the Mission officially took place. The story of the prayer triplet scheme is told in *Three Times Three Equals Twelve* by Brian Mills (Kingsway, 1986).

Light in Every Street ('LES') followed on from the prayer triplet scheme. Christians were encouraged to make their homes focal points of Christian witness, to help neighbours in practical ways and in prayer, until every street, town, village and towerblock in the UK had an identifiable Christian focus.

Ruth Calver is the mother of four children. She is an active member of ICTHUS Christian fellowship in South London, where she leads OASIS, a womens' prayer group. She is also involved in the local Parent Teacher Association (PTA), has her own speaking ministry, and is married to Clive, who is General Secretary of Evangelical Alliance.

6. Going It Alone

In spite of the massive breakdown of marriages and family life, on the whole women are still conditioned to believe that the greatest fulfilment and highest goal is to be found in marriage. TV advertisements, sermon illustrations, the Family Service—all reinforce the view that marriage is the norm. It is not surprising therefore that the unmarried often ask, 'Where do I fit in?' How the Christian Gospel becomes Good News to single people remains a challenge we have yet to meet.

Different Needs

It is easy to think of the unmarried as one group, and to assume that all their needs are the same. But being single at 30 is different from being single at 20 or 50, just as being a single parent or a widow differs from being someone who has never married.

One woman wrote to me recently:

> I am 50 and single. I have a responsible secretarial job and also have my elderly father living with me since he had a mild stroke last year. I never set out to be a 'career woman'. My desire for my life was marriage and a family. But this never materialised: relationships failed to develop. I have seen my contemporaries marry, have children and now even becoming grandparents—while I feel trapped in a permanent non-person limbo. I feel I need help in dealing

positively with my situation. Is there a like-minded group, a 'singles anonymous' which I could join?

Another admitted:

> I have found being single increasingly difficult. I am 31. My fiancée was killed in a road accident ten years ago. I never imagined that I wouldn't have met anyone else ten years later. I am still a virgin, believing that sex is a gift to be given in marriage and not before, even if it's a gift I never make. Ideally, I would like to marry a Christian who has never married before and who is interested in the arts. I might as well be asking for the moon. Sometimes I think my single-ness will go on forever.

While older single women struggle to come to terms with their lack of family and the emotional demands of caring for elderly relatives, younger women can easily get caught up in a whole succession of relationships, mistaking intimacy for commitment. Others hold such a high view of marriage that they are afraid of taking the risk of getting to know someone in case it doesn't work. Ultimately, what every single person seeks are relationships which can be trusted, where real communication takes place and where she is not over-admired or pitied because she hasn't 'made it to the altar'.

Judge Not

Single people do not have a spouse with whom they can share confidences and 'wash their dirty linen'. They have to find different support systems. Within the Church, this can be especially hard. Many single women have said to me that they have ended up by feeling a counselling case and a 'long-term problem' because they have shared some of their deepest anxieties with church people who don't seem to understand. It is not easy for married and single people to understand the particular stresses and strains they separately face. It's easy to judge and secretly assume that the grass is always greener on the other side of the fence.

Usually this is not the case. Finding ways of breaking down barriers between single and married women will usually take time.

Morals

Accepting single people *as they are* is important. Most non-Christians will not have Christian morals, though will probably be insulted if you infer that they don't have any. There will always be those who do not want to change, but many do, and it's best to let them come to that point themselves.

One woman admitted:

> I've always enjoyed my freedom—it's the best thing about being single. Sometimes I get lonely, but there are always things to do and I seem to have no trouble making relationships with men. It's OK if you're prepared to go to bed with them, but after a while, I get bored with the same old routines. I must say, just lately, I've begun to wonder what it's all about.

While women like this may feel initially condemned by church people, those who have made friends with Christian people have been really grateful for their practical help and commitment. In some cases, the friendship has helped them to become Christians. Sue admitted:

> I was amazed just how accepting Liz was of my situation, even though she was a Christian. I knew she couldn't possibly have approved of the kind of life I used to lead before my daughter was born, but she kept on supporting me. She had an inner strength I envied. When she told me her story, and all the ways that knowing Jesus made a difference to her life, I wanted that for myself.

At the end of the day, single people need to be reassured that sexuality is God's gift, not an assault course to achieve holiness! Here as in every area of life, we sin and need to know the cleansing power of Christ's blood and the power of forgiveness. This indeed is Good News for those who are already acutely aware of their failings and weaknesses.

Lesbians?

It can no longer be assumed that all single women are heterosexual. Whether by orientation or choice, increasing numbers are coming out and declaring themselves to be lesbian. While it is wrong to assume that all single women must be lesbian because they haven't married, there are those who find that a close emotional relationship with another woman is more supportive and fulfilling than previous experiences with men. This needs to be understood, though given the Church's traditional teaching on the subject, it is not surprising that many Christian women (single and married) find it difficult to accept lesbian women in their midst. Some have admitted to feeling emotionally threatened themselves. 'Suppose she wants a lesbian relationship with me,' said one Christian. It is easy to become so defensive that you fail to think of a lesbian as an individual for whom Christ died. Just as a married woman fears that her husband might go off and have an affair with a single girlfriend who is often in her home, so others shy from the responsibility of befriending a lesbian saying, 'If my husband knew I had a lesbian friend, it might affect our marriage.' Some Christian women need to come to terms with their fear of lesbianism if they are going to be at all effective in sharing the Good News with other women. The Bible teaches us to hate the sin and to love the sinner. There is no need to compromise on this, but to reject the person because of her practices is to go contrary to the teaching of Jesus, who accepts everyone without distinction.

The Dilemma of the Single Woman

It is wrong to assume that to be married is normal and that to be single as an adult has to be accounted for. However, there are other issues that single women face, issues that need to be recognised and respected. Actually getting involved in their world often demands getting rid of all kinds of wrong assumptions. Those single women who seem capable, well dressed, and a bit of a threat have vulnerabilities just like anyone else. 'I was amazed to find that Sandra was just like me underneath it all,' said Carol, a married friend of mine.

Whether she likes it or not, a single woman is her own breadwinner. Usually she has to support herself financially, as well as run a home, cook her own meals, wash clothes, shop and at some level, extend hospitality to others. It is easy to think that because she has no children, she has masses of spare time. In most cases this is simply not true. One woman said: 'I leave home at eight am and get back at six pm. By the time I've got myself something to eat, tidied up and made a few phone calls, it's almost time to go to bed to make sure I get enough sleep to get up in time to face the next working day.' In contrast, a married friend commented, 'I don't know how people cope with a nine-to-five job in the summer. I think I'd sign off in May until September.' Unfortunately that's just not possible!

A single woman is not, as some think, trying to compete in a man's world. Whatever her work, she is simply earning her living.

Childlessness

For the single woman, childlessness may become a major issue. Even if relationships with men have gone wrong, a woman who hears the biological clock ticking and knows her childbearing years are running out faces hard choices. Increasing numbers of single women are parents by choice, usually finding out afterwards just how tough it is to bring up a child single-handed. Thus it is more than likely that we may meet many non-Christian women who have children. The local church is usually less sympathetic when such women are actually members of a Christian body—perhaps their own—but this double standard should not exist. For as long as marriage is reinforced as the norm, and true

womanhood equated with motherhood, we cannot be surprised when single women marry divorcees or end up by
having children. Pam said to me:

> I got to the stage where I would rather have someone to care
> for than no one at all. I don't mind looking after other
> people's children, but it's not the same as having your own.
> Lucy is often a real handful, and at times it's difficult to get
> out and meet people, but I don't regret having her.

Good News for Single People

The single person who feels the pain and emotional empti-
ness of being single, can be helped to understand that the
crisis and challenge of being single is the crisis and challenge of being yourself. Everyone, whether married or
single, is faced with basic human questions: Who am I? what
am I here for? and to whom do I belong? For the single
woman these can become particularly acute, especially
when so many women take their identity from their husband and children or the man for whom they work. 'If I am
not "wife" "mother" "Mr Smith's assistant", then who am I?'
said one woman.

The Good News here is that our value in God's eyes does
not depend on marital status, or role relationships in relation to men. Everyone is loved equally by God, whether
married or single, male or female. More to the point, at the
heart of our faith is a God who chose to live out his life on
earth as a single person. While recognising the good gift of
marriage, Jesus also knew how easily family ties and responsibilities could obstruct the real issues of the Kingdom. In
God's scheme of things, marriage is not the ultimate goal
and seal on adult maturity. Many of our churches have got it
wrong, although some do offer the unconditional welcome
to all, which is so much at the heart of real Christian living.

Jesus knew what it was like to be single, and there is
nothing single people experience which is unknown to him.
All his life he had a special empathy for all who were outside

the system. Born in a stable and crucified between two out-
laws, he also died outside the city walls. For those who feel
the oppression of their singleness and separateness from
the 'normal' world of couples and families, Jesus knows
what it is like, and points towards a new order where there
will be no marriage.

The Good News is also that He also promises to be with
us—always. This promise, given to every believer, is
especially important to the single woman who has to face
life's many changes and stages on her own. A relationship
with Jesus offers that basis of identity and security which no
one person this side of heaven can provide.

God does guide. A single woman who has no partner to
make decisions with can be assured that God will guide her
through life, helping her to make wise decisions and choose
the best pathway for her life, even though she may not fully
see it at the time.

She need not fear barrenness. Although childlessness can
be a great deprivation, which must not be minimised, single
women in relationship to God can live exciting and creative
lives in a whole host of different ways. The Good News of
the Gospel is this: childlessness is not a stigma in God's
Kingdom, but an opportunity for a different kind of fruitful-
ness.

Practical Ways of Helping

While there are unique ways in which God reveals himself
to us individually, there are practical ways through which
we can be his hands and feet to single women known to us:
by taking an interest in the single woman's job, genuinely
recognising its stresses and strains; accepting her hospitality
and not presuming that a home is only a real home where
there are children; taking seriously relationship problems,
especially the depression of loneliness and the fear of beginning again, after having been hurt. We can help her to move
house, decorate, put up shelves, unblock drains and gene-

rally respond to domestic crises when they occur. Perhaps we can be sensitive to financial needs if big bills come unexpectedly (single women have no wedding presents to help them set up home and often little capital). Other ways of helping include being in touch enough to know if she is ill and needs someone to shop and cook a meal; encouraging women on their own to maintain their own transport for independence and safety reasons, especially when out on their own at night; offering to install special safety locks on doors and windows; being willing to be phoned in the middle of the night after 'obscene' phone calls if they happen. Single friends are usually more prepared to respond in these kind of emergencies, even to come and stay for a few nights if it helps. We should also be sensitive to festivals, eg, Christmas, Easter and Bank Holidays, which can be especially lonely.

Reaching out to single women means enjoying their company, finding out what makes them tick. If we arrange to do things together—shopping, listening to music, going to a film, sharing a meal—our friendship will be deepened.

Working it Out

Problems of identity and vocation, relating to others and finding out where our ultimate security lies are not worked out overnight. However, life is a gift given to each of us, and we must encourage each other to use it to the full, whatever our circumstances. Although single women have particular needs, not all may want to work them out among other singles. The nitty gritty of family life among married friends for many remains an important part of experience. Each single woman has her own story and is finding her own way of coming to terms with her lot as it is. We should respect that and encourage it. We must never try to force anyone into a mould. Our lives should not be uniform if they reflect the One who created the world in all its amazing variety! Single women need to see that their God is loving, dependable, demanding and life-affirming. Whether we are married or single, whether or not we turn to him in our times of joy and crises will make all the difference.

Kathy Keay

7. Single Parents

'I am going away for the weekend and I don't know if I am coming back.' It was ten o'clock on a Thursday night just after Christmas, and my husband John was speaking.

I sat still and quiet on the settee, my head pounding and my thoughts racing. Finally, I said, 'Where are you going?'

'To stay with Mary,' John replied.

'You don't need to say anything else,' I answered. Suddenly everything fell into place. All the previous weeks of tension, deception, bewilderment, pain, became as clear as daylight; he was leaving me for someone else. I was amazed at my calm exterior.

'Please God, keep my mouth shut,' I prayed.

He went on, 'I'm going to live with Mary at the weekend and come to work during the week. Don't talk about vows and duties; God wants me to be happy. I'm leaving in the morning, but don't tell anybody. I suppose you want me to sleep somewhere else.'

'I don't care where you sleep,' I retorted, 'but the boys will ask questions.'

We went to bed, I in a daze, he for the last time in that house. Next morning I awoke early and decided I couldn't stay to watch John leave. I got up and dressed, instructing Andrew, aged nine, and Mark, aged six, to do the same. Hurriedly, I pushed as many of their new toys as I could into a couple of bags. As I telephoned for a taxi, John came into the kitchen.

'I can't watch you go,' I said, 'but I am coming back to this house today.' He said nothing, but turned and began to pack. The boys and I stood in the hall, waiting. The taxi drove up, John said, 'Goodbye,' and we were off.

We arrived all in a mess on my parents' doorstep. I was plied with cups of tea while Dad played with the children and I tried to repeat what had happened.

Gone for Ever

There I was, 14 weeks pregnant, with two small boys, and my husband John (not his real name) was leaving me after over ten years of apparently happy marriage. I began to realise that I was regaining a sense of peace after the awful premonition I had had for the last few weeks that something terrible was going to happen. The physical pain had gone— so severe only the previous day that it had knotted my stomach and made it almost impossible to eat. Mum and Dad came with me on the bus back home. It was strange to walk back into the house—John was gone. Everything about him had gone. I walked in and out of all the rooms: the radio, one of his favourite things, had gone, the photo of the boys with Father Christmas wasn't in its place, his clothes from the wardrobe, the pyjamas from the bed. I knew, in reality, that John was gone and gone for ever. I tried to explain that Daddy had gone away for a while, but Andrew asked God to bring him back and I just cried.

As I sat alone in our double bed, I threw the pillows next to me across the room and I covered the empty space with books and magazines to help me through the night. I tried talking to God, and as I did I felt his arm round my shoulders. I was never to feel quite so alone again.

I quickly learned to function on several levels in order to meet the needs of the boys, and to keep my emotions as quiet and numb as possible. I telephoned a friend, a member at church, and tried to explain what had happened. He spoke lovingly to me and assured me again and again of

God's love for me and for my children.

'You know, Christine, God can use this,' he said.

'No, he can't,' I screamed. How could God use all this? I was a complete and utter failure; my Christian marriage in a mess, and I was unable to face the next hour, let alone days and months and years.

Friends Who Cared

Word of what had happened soon spread, and friends started to phone or visit. It was their reactions I found surprising. Many of our friends had been made through John and his work, and when he left I felt there must have been so much wrong with me that no one would like me. When friends came and showed that they cared, helping and giving practical support, I was deeply touched. This enabled me to take a big step towards normality. When John left, we had nothing ready for the new baby, just a shawl and a treasure-cot that I had kept for sentimental reasons. Now I had no money but, wonderfully, so many things arrived for this new child: cot, pram, pushchair, clothes, baby bath, blankets—everything that a small baby would need. This was how Andrew, Mark and I found we could see the Lord caring for us; he was in control whatever seemed to be happening at the time.

For the first few weeks, we didn't hear from John at all, although we knew where he was, and then we had a letter asking if he could take Andrew and Mark away for the weekend. It was agreed, after some considerable correspondence, that it would be better if they saw him just for a few hours one day. That day, while the boys were out, I felt I couldn't leave the house. Isabel, a Christian friend with great imagination, travelled some distance to be with me. The afternoon passed very slowly. As the boys went to bed that night, Andrew started to ask,

'Why does little Paul, the lady's son, call our Daddy "Daddy"? Why has Daddy taken off the ring you gave him?

Why does Daddy say you made him ill? If Daddy loved us, why would he leave us?' That was one question I couldn't answer. I tried to show them that I loved them, and finally they went to sleep. I went downstairs and cried as I had never cried before. I seemed engulfed in darkness.

After a long time, and joining me in tears, Isabel said quietly, 'There must be something we can thank God for.' There, as I sat in the armchair, we slowly started to count. Yes, the boys had come back. Yes, the baby was still all right inside me. With tremendous effort, I managed to list eight things I could thank God for.

Isabel prayed; I couldn't join with her, but I started to look up, and I never felt so low—so at the bottom of a pit—again.

After six months of being a single parent, I gave birth to a baby girl. Months of uncertainty and last-minute concerns for the safety of the baby gave way as she arrived, just before midnight. Truly I had seen God's protecting hand upon both our lives, and named her Victoria: the victory was the Lord's. I was now the proud mother of two sons and a daughter.

Many things happened over the next year or so: the visits to solicitors, dealings with affidavits, with law courts, barristers and registrars and a judge. We went to live with my parents and gained a vestige of stability. Life began to return to something like normality on the outside, but the inside turmoil was still with me. Slowly, too, I was beginning to learn to give God the feelings that I had: failure, anger, guilt, bitterness. How wisely I had been counselled not to let bitterness grow, to give it all to God as it started.

Many friends and family had prayed, visited and phoned. However, one friend, Jenny, had herself experienced something similar. She was unable to help in many of the other ways; she had a full-time job and three boys to raise on her own. But she had a special understanding of how I felt. It didn't need a lot of words, but it was very reassuring to me that I was normal. Also it was encouraging to see that she was a little further along the road and that she was succeeding—perhaps I could too.

Do Something

While we were both away at a parish weekend conference, we met other Christian single parents and found this contact encouraging, sharing some of the problems and feelings we had in common. Later one evening, standing in the corridor outside my room, we spoke of the help that such contacts had been, and also of the need to share about our situation with the wider Christian family.

Jenny said, 'Christine, you should do something.' I recalled those earlier words, 'Christine, the Lord can use this,' but I didn't want to hear, and I did nothing.

A couple of months later I was given a copy of a recently published *Family* Magazine. In that issue there was a letter from another single parent containing a plea, 'Are there any other Christian single parents out there? I'd love to meet up with them.' I answered that letter and I went to visit Melanie. We then had contact with other single parents and with Dr Anne Townsend, then Editor of *Family* Magazine. It emerged that we all needed something, and as we shared together, a vision came to me of an organisation that would link Christian single parents with others, especially those from a small fellowship. Perhaps we might also explain better to others something of our situation. I began to share this vision with all my friends for their prayers and advice. One morning I asked a friend to pray for a name for 'it'; later that day I was telling Anthea, a Christian single friend, about the idea. As I spoke she picked up a pencil and a piece of paper and wrote 'CLASP'— Christian Link Association of Single Parents—and CLASP was born.

When I went home that evening, Tony (another Christian single parent) had called to see my parents, and I excitedly shared this with them. We talked about a symbol, and Tony left to visit an artist who lived just down the road. He returned several days later with our symbol, two hands clasped over the cross. A few days later, I met Molly, an older single parent, and she handed me a £5 note.

'You'll be needing some funds,' she said, and this was the beginning of the Lord's supplying the means to start such a work—long before I had even thought of asking him for it.

By newsletter, we contacted everyone who might be interested, including those single parents I had already met, and the many Christian friends and contacts we had made over the years. It seemed right to get a small group together, perhaps to have a committee. Our first meeting was almost a disaster; CLASP nearly died on the spot! Many doubts and anxieties were expressed, but two of us felt that God was leading us in the right direction. We didn't do anything for a few weeks, but God wouldn't let us get away with it. The vision and calling returned. We joined with two other Christian single parents to form a National Committee. We were certainly filled with a vision, and far more enthusiasm than experience. Together we worked out some aims and the basis of faith, using the Evangelical Alliance's basis as a guide. God protected us from many of the potential mistakes we might have made. We had great fun in those early days as Barbara, Ann, Tony, David and I shared together and tried to find the way in which God was leading us to work specifically for him.

CLASP

A new organisation evolved. Membership is open to anyone who is a Christian single parent for whatever reason. Our aims are:

1. To provide Christian support for single parents and opportunities to share blessings and difficulties.
2. To link Christian single parents together, either in small groups or as individuals to CLASP.
3. To offer help to those suddenly facing single parenthood.

It was suggested that to put CLASP on a firm footing we

should be registered as a charity with the Charity Commissioners. This took some working out and the help of a solicitor. We appointed three trustees to offer advice and pastoral support; one is a member of the National Committee, one is a pastor married with children, and the third a doctor (herself a single parent).

One of the immediate results of the formation of CLASP was a deluge of letters. We found there were many people hurting, and they all needed to know that someone else understood. Hundreds of letters continue to pour in each year. Each one is answered personally, although usually I dictate replies, and a growing band of secretaries types them. Through the traumas, some people find it hard to believe that God is with them. We seek to assure them that God understands and loves them. Other letters tell of the most harrowing tragedies, but testify to God's faithfulness and of a deepening awareness of his strength and power in individual lives. Advice and practical suggestions are sought on all aspects of single parenthood. Here, many of my own experiences and those of others have been invaluable in identifying with the problems and seeking solutions. The following extracts are taken from a typical day's postbag:

'Could you please send me a form. I am a divorced lady with a three-year-old son. I am a Christian.'

'Money is a major problem, and I pray that the car will keep going without service or repair and that nothing will need repair in the home.'

'I am writing to ask if you will pray for me . . . At first I was given tremendous strength from the Lord to cope; now I am always so upset. I long to be loved and yet fear any involvement. Do you know of anyone who has been healed of such deep hurts? I try to be outward-looking but feel torn up inside. Please write back.'

'I am a single parent, a Christian with a 16-month-old daughter. I am 20 years old and just beginning to go through divorce. I feel that no one understands, no one cares or bothers to take an interest. I feel I just can't cope. I need someone to understand.'

'This summer was my time for being angry, angry with God for letting my husband die.'

'We are still receiving wonderful support from friends, but as the date of a Court hearing for custody gets closer, I feel fear . . . My best wishes and sincere thanks for all your help.'

Much prayer is offered as these letters are received and replies typed. All our helpers give their skills and time voluntarily. Some have stayed with us for a few months, others for years. All have shared in the sufferings of others and feel a special call to help in this way. Mostly we have worked from my home. Initially everything was contained in carrier bags! Now we have equipped an office in our local church. If a person wishes to become a member, she or he receives our newsletters three times a year. Almost all members ask to be linked with others in their area. Strong friendships have grown from these contacts, which sometimes develop into a local group. We suggest that a leader or committee registers with us to become an official CLASP group. This is often a means of evangelism as other single parents join in. From our mailbag today:

'I have made contact with the local branch of CLASP, which has been a great help.'

'Our group is going from strength to strength. It is wonderful to see the Lord's healing hand move amongst his damaged flock. We meet twice a month; the adults for prayer and praise, and every third Saturday have a family afternoon.'

'Our group meets only occasionally; we have had much help from each other, and are now able to stand alone and become more involved in our local fellowship.'

Much of the ministry of CLASP is involved in restoring a hurt person to wholeness in Christ. We rejoice when we are no longer required, although we welcome those who stay to help another person further along the road.

Our newsletters contain a pot pourri of items to help and uplift. They are a means of sharing news, book reviews, conferences, house parties, testimonies and specific requests for praise and prayer.

'Thank you for your last newsletter—reading them always creates a calm oasis in a busy day.'

'How lovely to have something that isn't a bill; I feel a link with you all and pray for you as I read the newsletter.'

'Your newsletter arrived on a day when I was feeling especially down.'

Newsletters are sent not only to members, but to all who are interested in our work. Some of our wider Christian family become 'Friends of CLASP' and seek to offer practical and financial help. Without their monetary giving this ministry could not continue. Without their prayer support we would all be poorer in many ways.

Early in 1983 some of us attended the first weekend organised specifically for single parents at Lee Abbey, North Devon. We were so encouraged that we decided to plan our own houseparties. God showed his unfailing love to us. From nowhere, it seemed, people have come to form the large teams we need to look after children from 0 to 16, as well as to minister to the adults. Our 'Friends' pray for the team and guests by name. We have seen lives changed by God. Joan is one. She arrived looking drawn and exhausted, two uneasy children by her side. She spoke in mono-syllables and everything was too much of an effort. Clearly this woman and her children would be difficult for us all— the team prayed hard that night! By the end of her stay with us, Joan was unrecognisable, the strain had eased, and she could laugh and share with us. Her children, too, reflected her newfound peace: 'I have not felt so loved in the four years since my husband died.'

We can reach only a small number of people by house-parties, so we also organise some day conferences. These look at specific aspects of our lives and again provide oppor-tunities for us to meet together. Anger, fear, facing the future, coping with the children are all topics we have dis-cussed. Our reactions are affected by what we believe and have been taught as Christians. Anger, resentment and guilt are emotions that we need to face up to and allow God to

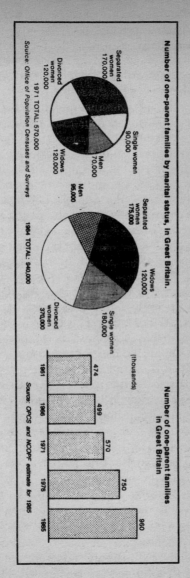

Number of one-parent families by marital status, in Great Britain.

1971 TOTAL: 570,000

Separated women 170,000
Single women 90,000
Men 70,000
Divorced women 120,000
Widows 120,000

Source: Office of Population Censuses and Surveys

1984 TOTAL: 940,000

Separated women 175,000
Men 95,000
Widows 120,000
Single women 180,000
Divorced women 370,000

Number of one-parent families in Great Britain

(thousands)

1961	1966	1971	1976	1985
474	499	570	750	960

Source: OPCS and NCOPF estimate for 1985

deal with. This often involves listening and counselling, frequently by phone. Our church fellowships often make a brave attempt to help. We are sure that the desire to assist is there, but the understanding is more difficult. Thus we welcome the opportunity to share with our wider Christian family something of what it is like to be a single parent. Members of the National Committee and local members have written articles, taken part in conferences and addressed church groups.

It is being involved in the lives of people like Joan, that thrills us. Our ministry is an ongoing one, as parenthood doesn't go away! (One of our older members calls herself a 'single granny'.) Sadly, the number of single parents continues to rise dramatically. By far the largest number come as a result of the breakdown of a marriage. One in three marriages in the UK ends in divorce. (See diagram.) The total number of children involved in divorce proceedings was 155,740 (50,265 under 4; 57,664 aged 5-10; and 47,811 aged 11-15, according to the Office of Population Censuses and Surveys). Recently, I sat outside our local County Court with another CLASP member. Fifty divorce cases were being 'rubber stamped' that morning. This is repeated every week all over the country. We have not yet come across a church fellowship which does not have a single-parent member. It is reckoned that everyone reading this chapter knows at least one single parent in their immediate family, church fellowship or neighbourhood. All single parents have been hurt. We all bear the scars of bereavement and pain, and the responsibility not only for our own lives, but for those of our children. It is a daunting task but one in which the whole Church can be involved.

I am aware of having been blessed by the love of so many who have enabled me to accept God's healing in my life. It is our prayer that you, too, will join with us in ministering to other single parents.

Just to add a romantic footnote, some years ago I married Tony, another single parent, and we share our home with five of our children. We also work together in the ministry of CLASP.

Suggestions for Helping Single Parents

Early Days

The first days and weeks following a separation or death are very difficult, and the experience is often shattering. These days can go by in a daze with an inability to grasp what has happened, regardless of previous arguments, bitterness or even violence. A relationship has been broken, and the grief is deep and real. Emotions of all sorts are running high. Initially come shock, numbness, and tears leading to anger, resentment, and more tears. Possibly this is a time to go and listen, say very little, listen again, make a cup of tea, just sit and be there. In a day or two it may be necessary to help with shopping, children, school, meals. It is also helpful at this point to be practical in helping with day-to-day tasks. It can be a difficult time to give explanations to the children, the parents or to in-laws in the wider family. Asking if you can help in these communications may also be appreciated.

Loneliness

Another adult once shared a large part of someone's life; he or she was there listening and talking. Now there is no one and the loneliness begins to grow. Perhaps it is at this stage that someone can begin to relate more deeply to the single parent. Take time to ask how the person is and mean it, not necessarily at church after the service, but when there is time for the person to have a good talk and perhaps a good cry. Be careful: children have very big ears, so pick your time. Single parents need help, but can't or won't always ask. It is difficult for single parents to communicate this to other people. It is often hard for them to receive, and they need to go through a process of learning how. Responses may come out negatively, coloured by the bitterness of the moment,

resentments relating to what has happened, and the tired-
ness of perhaps months of difficult home relationships and
constantly demanding children. Single parents very often
feel rejected, desperately inadequate and not only physically
but emotionally tired. They can feel physically unattractive,
too, and are quick to detect even the slightest hints of rejection. The single parent has to appear to have it 'together', to
put on a brave face, because of the need to get through from
morning to night. What was once dependency on another
person, by necessity, seems to drift into independence
fraught with its own dangers.

Evenings

It is often when the children are in bed and the house is
empty and lonely that the overwhelming effects of being a
single parent seem at their height. Telephoning, particularly
in the evening, is of great importance and encouragement.
However, don't be surprised if the person spends time
being silent, either frightened of breaking down, or saying
too much. To phone and give encouragement at that time of
day can be particularly helpful or, if possible, a visit in the
evening.

Decisions

Decisions have to be made in many important areas being
faced alone by the single parent. First, you can help by
listening and then by gently giving advice or pointing the
person in the right direction; children, house, finance,
school, legal matters are all areas where decisions were
often made by two people, and now have to be made by
one. The world of solicitors, magistrates, social services,
DHSS, court room, probate, wills, etc, are frightening to
most of us, and more so if we are facing them by ourselves.
This is a practical area where the Christian can draw alongside, and accompany the single parent, particularly when
they go to court (which often involves a great length of time
sitting outside while the person is inside). You can be there

to hear them and support them after the court's decisions
have been made.

What About the Children?

All the children involved in a single parent family have been
affected by the tragedy of breakup, bereavement or illegit-
imacy. It may seem that single parents do not take their
sorrow enough into account, as they are coping so much
with their own difficulties—practical and emotional. Very
often a single parent can appear short-tempered and im-
patient with them, or unable to discipline them. This is a
particularly sensitive area, but one where the wider
Christian family can help—perhaps, most of all, to include
them in family outings, or to take them away for a little
while, just a break of an hour or two. This is valuable to all
parents, but particularly to the single parent. It allows
children to mix, to see the normality of another Christian
home.

Perhaps, instead of criticising, we can show by example in
our own homes, how children can be better helped and
guided. In fact, in the whole area of bringing up children,
there is much with which other members of the wider
family can help. With small toddlers, it may involve just playing, talking, and taking an interest in the things they do. We
must remember that there isn't a Dad or Mum to show the
things that they bring proudly from school. Whether we are
male or female, we can bring something of the father or
mother figure to a child who has lost a parent. Children of a
single mother particularly miss being carried on their
father's shoulders. As the children grow older, there may
not be the opportunity to do things with Dad such as rough
and tumbles, football and fishing. Conversely, a single
father, particularly if he has daughters, needs female help—
taking a daughter to the toilet, advice on menstruation, the
first bra, fashion, etc. Usually these things pass naturally
from mother to daughter, but they may not happen so easily
when there is only a father present. These are ways in which

another family can be of help, and also single members of the church who do not have the responsibilities of a family of their own, who could become an adoptive granny, auntie or uncle. Remembering birthdays and Christmas and the little things that are so difficult for the single parent to provide are all important.

Teenagers desperately need people with whom they can talk. Talking to parents is often difficult, even more so when there has been a split. They need to be able to feel safe enough to vent the feelings they are unable to vent at home. Many are very sensitive to the things that have happened and don't want to upset the parent that they live with more than they need to. Often they won't say how they feel about the absent parent, for example about going to see them, or some of the smaller things that seem so large in their own lives. So we need to befriend the teenagers, too.

Custody

One enormous area of conflict for many single-parent families is that of access, the term used where children see or visit the non-custodial parent. Very often the arrangements are the result of court decisions because the parents involved have been unable to make a compromise decision of their own. Often there has been an enormous amount of bitterness over court procedures. The parent with whom the child lives feels under enormous pressure, and the strain of thinking about the children going to stay with the parent who has hurt them so much is difficult and complicated.

This is where someone can draw alongside the custodial parent (the parent who has the child all the time) and be with him or her during the period of access when the children go away. Although there are times when all parents long to break from their children, it is also true that when circumstances are fraught, they do not want to see the children go. The single parents feel they have lost so much that they are frightened of losing the children as well. They have been hurt by the absent partner, and are frightened that the children are going to be hurt too. Of course, children usually are affected by arrangements of access. Even when legal proceedings have gone most smoothly, they are still affected by the strain involved in the change of house, different rules, different situations, and the trauma of leaving the other parent again. This can lead to the saddest situation, when the children are physically or mentally affected to such an extent that there is great emotional disturbance. So if it is possible, we must try to be with the parent while the child is away so that he or she is not left to think about it alone. We can arrange to go out together, or, if they feel they can't leave the house—as is quite frequently the case—stay together in the house and suggest activities that will help to keep the mind occupied as much as possible during this difficult time. If possible, we should be there before the child goes, in order to help during the difficult couple of hours before the absent parent arrives to take the child away.

Similarly, you may know the person who is the non-custodial parent, and who has the children to stay. He may be unfamiliar with the child now, because of not living together all the time. If it is the father, as is so often the case, he is not always sure how to look after his children all the time, or what to do with them. Maybe here you can help him or give him some encouragement.

Hospitality

Offering hospitality is another important opportunity, and one that is not always considered. We all like to share with other people. It is particularly important for the single parent to have a break from routine and the pressures of getting every meal for children who generally don't appreciate what is cooked for them.

Finances

Finance can be a big worry to the single-parent family.

Almost always their income has dropped considerably from the one they were used to before. (Very occasionally, there are those who do find that they are better off, generally those who are widowed.) In the case of those who have suffered a marriage breakdown, their income drops by at least half. They still have not only themselves but their children to care for. Many, particularly because single-parent families are often headed by women, are not able to find employment, so the difficulty of making ends meet is severe. Many whom CLASP comes across are supported by the DHSS. Supplementary Benefit is just on the poverty line. Here there are two ways in which we can help: first, by helping fill in the forms. They need to see that they are claiming all possible benefits. If they pay tax, we should see that they are claiming the single-parent benefit allowance on the income tax they pay. Secondly, there is practical help, to meet their special needs where we can. Leave money in an envelope just before a bill, stamps for electricity, gas and the TV licence. Give vouchers, perhaps before a child's birthday so that the parent can buy a special treat; or leave a box of food on the doorstep when you know the cupboard is bare. Sometimes give some of the extras, the luxuries that we enjoy but they can't afford.

Holidays

Being faced with lack of income means generally an inability to go away on holiday or have a break. All of us appreciate a holiday. This is particularly so for those who have suffered the trauma of breakdown or of bereavement and need, therefore, to get away for a time on their own—away from their usual surroundings. There are a growing number of Christian organisations and opportunities for single parents to get away together, though costs can of course be a problem. In some cases the Christian organisations running the holiday are able to give a bursary if people apply for it, but very often it is the local church that helps to meet the needs by sending its single-parent family on holiday.

Domestic Help

If single parents are able to return to work, then of course, they are going to need help with the children, particularly during school holidays. This again is a time when the local church can offer to help.

Housing poses an even more serious question. Some single-parent families find that they are homeless, though not through direct fault of their own. There are those who fall into a group that is missed by the Local Authorities, for example, those who leave their homes because of violence. In many areas there are refuges for those who have been battered and for their children, but in many instances, they are overcrowded, and provision is not adequate for long-term stay. These people need help to find accommodation. For those who have left because the emotional pressure has become too great, with mental cruelty involved, and in some cases those whose house has come with the job, there is no alternative accommodation, and Council provision isn't always suitable or available. Some single parents go back to live with their own parents, taking their children with them. Clearly, this is far from an ideal situation, and involves a great many stresses. Here perhaps being alert and aware of the situation can be helpful and, again, providing the break, the hospitality that would help both the single parent and those with whom they are living.

On a long-term practical level, the single-parent family is going to need help with the care of its own house. For example, a woman may need help with house repairs, fitting in the new washing machine, changing the washer on a tap, mowing the lawn, replacing a roof tile, digging over the garden, or servicing a car—practical things that she may find difficult on her own. A man on his own with children may particularly appreciate someone cooking an extra cake, perhaps for a birthday or Christmas, or help with housework or mending.

Transport

We can also offer transport, particularly for getting to and from church and mid-week meetings, or to go out with them for the day—take them away from familiar surroundings, give them the opportunity to do things that many other families are able to do. Go with them, especially on outings, perhaps to the seaside for the day. It has been said that there is nowhere as lonely as a beach crowded with families when your own family is incomplete. Intimate family times like Christmas and Easter can be very lonely.

Spiritual Sensitivity

When it comes to the Christian faith, most single parents have taken a number of knocks both to their view of God and his treatment of them. Here, care and genuine concern for the person without judgement or criticism can be of great value. We can gently remind each other that whatever has happened, God loves us; he is with us. He won't let us go; he isn't affected by how we feel from time to time; he isn't shocked by our outbursts of anger and will always be there. We must pray for the single parent, but not expect him or her always to be able to pray in turn.

Occasionally, it may even be possible for a reconciliation to take place. We must never rule out the hand of God and the miraculous in such circumstances. While it would be wrong to raise false hopes and also wrong to dash the hopes that exist, it is a very delicate matter when two people decide to try again. They desperately need the love and support of those around them. Although it is rare to see this happen, and rare for it to work, sometimes people do try a second time, and may fail again. Their feelings are then even worse than the first time. Where it is possible for a true reconciliation to take place, they equally need the love, support and care of those around them.

Christine Tufnell

Christine Tufnell has worked as a teacher and playgroup supervisor and is now founder and national director of CLASP (Christian Link Association for Single Parents). She is married to Tony and has six children, five of whom live with her (three children are her own and three are step sons). The family is based in Chenfield, Essex.

8. Christianity and Feminism: Must We Choose?

The political 'me' wants responsibility and choice. The fantasy 'me' wants to be rescued. And the real-life 'me' just gets embarrassed about the muddle.

Sheila Rowbotham, *New Society* 1986.

Feminists are people for whom Christ died because of his love. There are feminists in the Western Church yet so far, the Church has not taken seriously the challenge of presenting those outside the Church with the Gospel. This is in spite of the fact that feminists still greatly influence society's thinking today. Of all the unreached people in the UK and USA, feminists outside the Church rank high on the list. It is rare to find feminists and Christians sitting comfortably together in one room, and many reading this chapter will have an inbuilt dislike for—even scepticism about—these women, not least because of popular media stereotypes. Nevertheless they remain, in many ways women like us, and potential sisters in Christ.

If it is true that many Christians are sceptical of feminists, it is also true that many feminists are sceptible of Christians and Christianity. Why is this? What are the feminist objections to Christianity? And how can feminists be presented effectively with the Good News of Jesus Christ? After all, the Church has generally been patronised primarily by women, why are some now so resistant? If the Gospel is not Good News for women of *all* kinds, then what is it? This chapter aims to help those who wish to understand feminists more clearly, and who genuinely want to understand them in order to communicate this Good News.

Julie was a journalist. She smiled at me as I settled into the coach seat next to her. It wasn't long before we started talking. She asked me what I did (a usual opening line but one which inevitably gave me the chance of introducing the Christian faith). After telling her that I worked for a Christian organisation, her expression changed. 'I would never set foot in a church,' she said. 'I want to be with people who will give me more power, not less,' she continued. Julie was intelligent and friendly. It emerged that she had been a churchgoer when she was young. As she grew older and started asking questions, no one in the church seemed able to answer them. Like so many other women I have met, Julie felt increasingly out of place in a set-up which seemed to expect all women to become wives and mothers, and to fit into church life without question. She had nothing against motherhood, but she felt that no one was interested in her for who she was. 'As I went week by week I felt more and more lonely,' she said. 'I couldn't help noticing that while the pews were full of women, all the activities were run by men. The more I looked into it, the harder I found relating Christianity to my being a woman. Eventually, I couldn't take it any longer, and left.'

Julie's case against the Church is not uncommon among feminists. Her desire for power wasn't as daunting as it may seem. To me, it simply showed that she was ambitious and wanted to get on in the world. It seemed to her that Christianity and the Church demanded that she should deny herself, her interests and personality just to fit into the Church. Christianity seemed to her to be for people, especially women, who didn't think too much or question what they were told: Christian women, it seemed, were to be subservient and happy for others to make the decisions for them. It wasn't usual for them to have a sharp social conscience or to be concerned with anything very much outside their immediate families and church activity. Was this what

Christ really demanded of women? I knew perfectly well from my own experience that this was not the case.

The Feminist Case Against God

In her book *Patriarchial Attitudes*, Eva Figes outlines what she believes to be the feminist case against God. She states:

> The voice of God is the voice of man. The male Jehovah is a stern Hebrew patriarch who leaves us in no doubt about the position of women. Far from being the mother of all races, the natural order has been reversed, and woman is born out of man—no more than a single male rib . . . The full responsibility of the Fall is heaped upon her shoulders. Just as Pandora let loose old age and vice, the evils of the world, so Eve was made responsible for man's mortality and fall from grace.[1]

This image of woman runs deep throughout Church history, and any feminist acquainted with it has good reason to ask if things have changed. On the position of women in the Church, Eva Figes writes, 'The Church may be dying on its feet, but it will cling to the last to the male exclusiveness which was its *raison d'etre* in the first place.' Current debates on the ordination of women and the possibility of a mass male exodus from the Church if this happens do nothing but harm to women who wish to become Christians and find their place within the Church. If feminists are to be won for Christ, they need to see other women spiritually alive and active within local churches—and this means far more than doing the flowers or leading the cleaning rota!

Who Is Feminist?

Not all feminists are educated, middle-aged women like Julie. Increasingly, they are to be found among women of every walk of life, including Asian and West Indian communities. There is no single united feminist voice today; in fact, within the contemporary feminist movement, there are several different groups—liberal, Marxist, and radical—as outlined by Elaine Storkey in her book *What's Right with Feminism?* [2] I would summarise her thinking as follows.

Liberal Feminism

Over the last fifteen years or so, the different voices of feminism have become more noticeable. Liberal feminists are most concerned about changing society to help women as individuals gain greater personal freedom. This has involved, among other things, tackling the economic exploitation of women through the trade union movement; campaigning for equal pay and the provision of childcare. Liberal feminism has been pushing for changes in legislation that will in any way improve the status of women and help secure their so-called 'right to choose', whether it be abortion on demand or to stay at home with the kids. Most Christians would take issue with some of the goals of the liberal feminists, but must sympathise with their aim of allowing women a choice.

Marxist and Radical Feminism

Women in these groups believe that passing a few laws, however important, is not enough. Even major changes such as women winning the vote are seen by them as only one tiny step towards equality in a society where the very structures of inequality and injustice remain. Socialist feminists believe that the class system, a capitalist economy like our own, and the power relationships which go with them, are all at fault and must be replaced.

Radical feminists on the other hand don't see socialism as the answer. For them, it's men who are the real oppressors, and socialist men can be just as bad as any other. Radical feminists believe that women need to dissociate themselves entirely from men. Both groups attack the family unit for keeping women and children dependent economically upon the male bread-winner, and for forcing women into an isolated domestic role, especially if she has small kids. 'I get really fed up stuck at home all day and there's something deeply humiliating about spending my husband's money' is a common complaint.

It's within the radical camp that lesbianism finds its strongest supporters, though not all feminists are lesbians and not all lesbians are feminists. Radical feminists however are among the first to point to the growing number of women suffering from rape and sexual abuse and to stress that sexual exploitation, even within marriage, is inevitable; they feel that this is true because men remain physically more powerful, and all too often find ways of beating, crushing and forcing women into submission. Women must reclaim their bodies, especially their reproductive powers, if ever they are to be free of men, say radical feminists. In some cases this could lead to transplanting the human embryo into the uteri of animals to free women from the sexual politics of men and from childbearing. Christians cannot accept this, but it is important to understand the roots of radical feminist thinking.

Thus each group of feminists expresses a different emphasis, though all are concerned to challenge traditional assumptions about women, their sexuality, their roles in society and in every area of life. Although lesbians are to be found in each group, radical feminists are by conviction lesbian, believing that the only answer way of overcoming patriarchy is to disassociate completely from men. Of course not all feminists would hold such views.

What Is Feminism?

In 1878 Millicent Garrett Fawcett said that 'Feminism has as its goal to give every woman the opportunity of becoming the best that her natural facilities make her capable of.' A hundred years later Devoki Jain said, 'Feminism is about women uniting as women to generate a force which presses society to accept and accommodate femaleness as equal even if different.' Both statements could be made by feminists today. For at the root of most contemporary feminist issues lies the human search for identity and vocation: Who am I? What am I here for, and how can problems relating to my sexuality, economic status and social roles be worked out here and now? These are the questions that many women feel the Church has failed to address. And whether Christian or agnostic, each of us carries heavy emotional baggage (assumptions and views from our own upbringing) which often prevents us from seeing the real issues clearly.

Patriarchy

Before trying to communicate the Gospel to feminists, it is important to understand that the 'underlying problem' they see in every society is patriarchy. They believe that everything is structured by men for men, whether it be within the home, in church, at work, within marriage or simply on TV.

The oppression women feel from patriarchal attitudes includes the way they are defined by men. Feminists—whether Christian or not—believe that what we understand as being 'feminine' is little more than what men have defined for us (and which the Christian tradition has generally upheld). This involves being seen to be sexually attractive to men, and behaving in a way that in no way challenges the popular macho image. Notice how—usually—women are congratulated when they look good, do the daily chores with a smile, and bolster a man's ego in a whole variety of ways. Yet as soon as she starts expressing her own views, or chooses an alternative wardrobe, some question her very femininity!

The whole area of gender definitions (ie, what it means to be male or female) is basic if we are going to understand feminism. All feminists would agree that these need to be redefined in order to liberate men as well as women. The way this expresses itself is different in each woman we meet. It is important therefore to listen carefully and allow a feminist to tell her story, so as not to jump to conclusions.

Feminist Origins

What has become known as the second wave of the feminist movement emerged largely from the protests of the sixties. Like American feminism in the 1830s, it developed from a deep disillusionment with values in British and American society. After the Second World War, women who had been the reserve labour force returned en masse to the home, where they were encouraged by powerful propaganda to buy up all the latest domestic gadgets and so fulfil their newly defined roles as wives and homemakers. Advertisements for soap, elaborate hairstyles and gadgets filled the growing number of women's magazines. Not that these ideas were bad or wrong in themselves; for many women they were a welcome change after the austerity of the war years. However, after a while, romantic images of love and marriage began to wear thin. Women began to withdraw into their own groups to express what American feminist Betty Friedan described as 'a problem without a name'.

In her book *The Feminine Mystique*, she wrote:

> It was a strange stirring, a sense of dissatisfaction, a yearning that women suffered in the middle of the twentieth century. Each suburban housewife struggled with it alone. As she shopped for groceries, made beds, matched slip cover material, chauffeured her children to boy scouts and brownies, and lay beside her husband at night—she was afraid to ask, even of herself, the silent question: Is this all?[3]

Most feminists today will have been through similar disenchantment before developing their own feminist convictions. No protest develops overnight, and feminists themselves should not be written off as a bunch of women who have 'got it wrong', or who are 'just a bit odd.' Christians need to take them seriously. Feminism in its different forms is deeply rooted in what has happened to women, individually and collectively over different eras. Often the strongest feminists are those who are most aware of the change, and among them are many women who have been exploited and deeply hurt by men and the system which they find themselves in.

It is often at this point—when Christians, whether feminist or not, meet feminists—that Christians withdraw, instead of bringing to them an understanding of Christ and his liberating Gospel. While society, and the Church is particular, still condition women to believe that our greatest fulfilment is to be found primarily in relation to men as wives and mothers, there will always be women who, whatever they are doing, will ask the question, 'Is this all?'

How Should Christians Respond?

Reaching feminists, then, involves listening to real questions which all Christians should take seriously. For example, you may be happy to be supported financially by your husband, but what if you are not married? What about those for whom unequal job opportunities mean they haven't enough money to support themselves and their dependents? Why is it that a large percentage of women workers are clerical and domestic workers, and generally still occupy the supportive role, while an equally large percentage of men remain in the top jobs?

Consider too, the sexual vulnerability of women. This may not apply to those who have a car or live in certain secure areas. However, in Lambeth (for example), the mugging rate (including rape) has risen to a record of 50 incidents per week. In most inner-city areas and elsewhere, women are afraid to go out alone whether during the day or night. Most feminists feel passionately about having to live, as it were, under a curfew, and few can afford cars. There are many practical ways in which by being sensitive to feminist issues it is possible to show the love of Christ to feminists themselves in a whole variety of ways.

For example, perhaps churches or women's groups within churches could use cars or hire mini buses as community transport services for women. Where faminist values predominate, it is largely up to women to reach out to other women and show them the reality of Christ in their lives. This means going into their world, understanding their issues, listening to them even if we don't agree. It means exchanging books with feminist friends; setting up small discussion groups—letting them decide the agenda; starting or joining a local prayer and support group with other sympathetic women in our area. We can suggest to our church the possibility of starting a crêche or nursery for the local community or a woman's help-line for rape crisis counselling and a regular Christian phone-in service. We cannot forget our homes of course, where friendships of trust can be made and confidences shared.

Motives, Not Rules

Most people are only prepared to listen to us when we have proved in practical ways that we care about them. Feminists are no exception. In understanding them, we cannot afford to be naive, but we need never be ashamed of being Christian and sharing the real basis of liberation through Christ with them.

Many feminists have felt trapped by traditional role expectations. They need to be told that very little is written in the Bible about male/female roles. Jesus cooked breakfast, talked to children and washed feet—all considered to be women's work at the time. The Bible talks more about people's motives and intentions than clearly defined roles for both sexes. Discovering this can be extremely liberating for feminists.

In God's Image

Men and women made in God's image have equal value before God (Gen. 1). When a feminist understands this, it can make a tremendous difference to the way she sees herself. She need never feel inferior to men, nor is she given grounds to dissociate from them. She can then understand that the development of patriarchy is largely a result of the Fall. All that was meant to be in terms of dignity and partnership between the sexes was spoilt by our human rebellion against God recorded in Genesis 3. The hurt, mistrust and exploitation which most feminists have experienced first hand are a direct result of the Fall. In the light of this, it is important to emphasise that the coming of Jesus radically affected the lives of women for good. For anyone wishing to illustrate this point, a study of Jesus' encounters with women in Luke's Gospel is well worthwhile as we saw in Chapter One of this book. In many meetings, even with the most radical feminists, most are extremely impressed with the way Jesus treats women, both within the Bible and in the lives of Christian women who are prepared to tell their own stories honestly today.

In the words of Dorothy Sayers,

> Jesus was a prophet and a teacher who never nagged at women, never flattered or coaxed or patronised. He never made jokes about them. He never mapped out their sphere for them, never urged them to be feminine or jeered at them for being female. He had no axe to grind and no uneasy male dignity to defend. He took them as he found them and was completely unselfconscious. There is no act, no sermon, no parable in the whole Gospel that borrows its pungency from female perversity. No one could possibly guess from the words and deeds of Jesus that there was anything 'funny' about a woman's nature.[4]

Without being glib, it is possible to communicate to feminists that Jesus still comes into individual lives to heal the hurt and deliver people from the long-term effects of any exploitation. Although Jesus never campaigned for women's rights, he did treat them with respect and a challenging graciousness that not only shattered prevailing sexist attitudes, but proved liberating in the truest sense.

The Source of Oppression

It is important to stress that although we may be hurt by

others, and feel rightly oppressed by unjust systems and legislation the real enemy we need to fight is not man, or the Church or institutions, but rather sin within the human heart—both male and female—and most of all within our own hearts. Social and political action can then take place, from a heartfelt concern to liberate others, motivated by Christ's concern rather than by anger or bitterness, as is sometimes the case. Once a feminist understands that we are all sinned against, and sinners, then it is possible to explain the heart of the Gospel. However, this is best communicated once the trust has been established. It is important to understand and respect the reasons why some women are feminists, and how they express that lifestyle in their individual lives.

It is important to realise, too, that feminists are basically no different from any other women. It is in being a woman and in talking from a woman's experience that the biggest link between Christian women and feminists outside the Church is forged. While some feminists are willing to listen to men, it is not so easy for men to gain the credibility necessary to communicate the Gospel to women. Both single and married women who feel an affinity with much of what feminists are saying have a unique opportunity to befriend them, and in so doing to introduce them to Jesus.

Questions of identity, sexuality, economic status and social roles are not worked out overnight, whether we are Christian women or not. However, if Jesus took time with tax collectors and sinners, and rebuked the religious people of his day for expecting him to mix only with those who were 'respectable', what right have we to disassociate ourselves from our feminist sisters and others today who may need him the most?

Historic Developments of the Women's Movement in the UK

What is the context and background for a Christian response

to feminism? It is helpful to encapsulate the history of the women's movement thus:

1792   First Major Publication: *The Rights of Women*, Mary Wollstonecraft.

Pre-Industrial Revolution—need to distinguish between women and class structure.

Working-class women: cottage industries move to factories.

Middle-class women: lifestyle largely created after the industrial revolution. Wealthy millowners bought large property away from work sites. The isolation of women in the home.

Upper-class women: taught to be strongly conscious of social responsibility towards the lower classes.

1841   Women removed from factory work.

1852   Quarter of female population working.

1865   The suffragette movement established.

1902   Women's Social/Political society formed civil disobedience as a means of direct access to Parliament.

1914–18   First World War. Working women's involvement in national employment.

1918–34   Women in employment and in home-roles fairly defined and accepted.

1928   Women given the vote.

1939–45   Second World War. State day nurseries provided to release women for employment.

1944   Education Act 'free' and compulsory education for both sexes.

1945–60   The quiet years, though intellectual activity continued.

1950s   Women 're-established' in the home.

1960s   Increasing developments in education and professions.

1960s   Women's Lib. *The Feminine Mystique*, Betty Friedan, 1963, and *The Captive Wife*, Hannah Gavron, 1966, exposed the position and frustrations of professional women at home.

1967–8   US influence in Great Britain.

1967   Abortion legalised in Great Britain.

1970   First National Women's Conference, Oxford.

           Proposals made: Equal pay for equal rights, 24-hour nurseries, Free contraception, Women's right to opt for abortion.

1972   First refuge for battered wives/women.

1974	Free contraception granted on NHS.
1975	Equal Opportunities Commission established to defend Sex Discrimination Act, 1974.
1976	First rape crisis centre set up in N. London.
1978	Last National Women's Conference held.
	Present split between Socialist and Radical feminists— no united feminist voice.

The need to know women closely and individually, to discern the issues.

The changing role of women has provided new opportunities for women, but at the same time has generated new pressures for both women and men.

How to Contact Feminists Outside the Church

Ideally, it is best to start with women we meet daily, either at work or at a regular meeting place, such as creche, work or school. However, a visit to the local women's centre can be useful. If we introduce ourselves as enquirers, we can learn about the women themselves and ask for a booklist and details of activities run on a regular basis. If it seems appropriate, we might ask one of the women how she became a feminist and what being a feminist means to her. There may be opportunity for us to say simply that we are Christians who are genuinely interested, which will no doubt come as somewhat of a surprise to the women there! Many of the meetings run by women's centres have become almost exclusively lesbian, and many Christian women do not want to attend these. However, it is usually possible to find one that is a more open, general meeting. Through these, we can get to know one or two other women personally. It is only then that there can be a basis for discussion and understanding.

Feminist workshops and conferences (Christian and non-Christian) are well worth attending, not only in order to learn, but in order to link with others who in time can become good friends. We should also become familiar with feminist books, and articles in magazines and newspapers which deal with feminist issues. Most of all, we need a sincere interest in the people we meet. Adequate prayer backing and support from other Christian friends is vital, and we must be prepared to learn as much as we give.

Kathy Keay

Notes

[1] Eva Figes, *Patriarchal Attitudes* (MacMillan: 1986).

[2] (SPCK: 1985).

[3] Betty Freidan, *The Feminine Mystique* (Penguin: 1985).

[4] Dorothy Sayers, *Are Women Human?* (Eerdmans).

9. Christian Viewpoint—
Christian Lunch and Dinner Clubs

For many years, throughout most of Britain, there have been groups of women concerned to meet together to pray for their friends and neighbours. They have planned to find ways of presenting the Christian Gospel to women often totally outside the traditional church scene. Knowing the appeal of an attractive meal to women only too glad not to think about cooking for once, local groups have often used meals as a focus for drawing women out of their homes and into an informal, unthreatening, welcoming atmosphere, where part of the time has been set aside for a simple presentation of the Christian Gospel. Until 1985 these groups were called 'Christian Lunch and Dinner Clubs'. They are now known as Christian Viewpoint.

The aim of this organisation among women is twofold: to bring non-Christian women to know Christ, using the acceptable social peer group of the local scene; and to link together such groups and provide fellowship, prayer backing, and conferences for training and encouragement. Each Christian Viewpoint group consists of a committee (normally from three to nine members), all of whom are required to be in agreement with an evangelical basis of faith. All committee members of groups affiliated to Christian Viewpoint must accept this.

An executive committee comprised of women with CV experience from around Britain meets three or four times a year to steer the work, to plan and pray together, aiming to provide back-up, know-how, and training conferences. In 1986, an official office and paid secretary became necessary to cope with the work load, and the organisation was given charitable status.

Though the work is largely among women, men are in some places included, and most groups plan some mixed outreach events each year. In areas of high unemployment and where there are retired folk, invitations are often given to men to join the women on a regular basis. Non-Christian women seem happy to come together for a couple of hours with friends to share food in a pleasant atmosphere, and to consider the reality of faith in Jesus Christ.

The majority of women serving on CV committees are married and generally aged 30-plus. Mothers of pre-school children are not as free as those whose children are at school, at college, or have left home. Thus the age of those who come largely depends on the age of the committee, since guests are normally the friends or colleagues of the committee members. Consequently, the majority of women reached are also in the 30-plus bracket, and the majority are married. But there are groups—for example Hayes (Kent) Mother and Toddler CV— which meet in the morning for coffee, organise a crèche, and mainly reach mothers with pre-school children.

How It All Began

Jean Rees of Hildenborough Hall, visiting America in the 1960s, was introduced to the work of Christian Women's Clubs. Inspired by what she saw, Jean returned to Britain and in 1967 called together a number of her female friends interested in evangelism. Over a Chinese lunch in the West End to which Ruth Graham (in London with Billy for the Earls Court Crusade) was invited, these women began to pray and plan for lunches to be held in London. With the chairing of Jean Rees, 'Christian Lunch and Dinner Clubs' was born. The idea was for the women to invite their friends to go up to town with them, perhaps to shop, and then take them as their guests to lunch.

During the lunch, some traditionally feminine interest feature would be presented—eg, ways with jewellery, model millinery, floral arrangements in winter. Then a speaker— usually female—would speak for 20–30 minutes on an advertised topic, inviting women to turn to Christ. Two lunches a year were held in London, until it became too expensive to continue. By this time, a larger group of Christian women had come to the lunches and caught the vision; they were beginning to pray and plan towards more local events. In its early days, most of the lunches or dinners were held in hotels or fairly smart restaurants, and the women who attended were exclusively those who felt at home in such surroundings—the materially privileged.

Ruth Graham became the first president; Marion Timmins became secretary; and Joyce McKechnie the treasurer. Marion and Joyce are both still active in the work of Christian Viewpoint, and it is their input, with God's help, that has led to the growth of the work. As well as pioneering lunches and dinners, the organisation planned to help already existing independent outreach groups among women to be linked together for mutual support and encouragement.

Information on speakers with a flair for communicating the Christian faith to non-Christian women was shared among these groups, and the first 'speakers' list' was compiled. The basis of faith was drawn up and a handbook produced to help new clubs get started. A three-monthly magazine to share news and encourage prayer support was introduced. Prayer and calculated risks went hand in hand, and women began to come to Christ in the CLDC movement.

Over the nearly 20 years of its existence, there has been visible growth, and at the time of writing over 150 groups are affiliated. Almost all of the new groups have come into being when women from a neighbouring area have come by invitation to a lunch—then caught the vision and become excited at the possibility of God doing such a work in their town or village. This has meant that in some areas a number of neighbourhood groups have started up reasonably quickly. For example, Sevenoaks—a typical high-income commuter town in mid-Kent —started to have lunches in a hotel there in 1972. A few years later other groups started up in Knockholt, St Mary Platt, Otford, Ightham and Plaxtol— all villages within a seven-mile radius of the initial starting point. Hundreds of women were being confronted with the claims of Christ. In the last twelve months, 23,000 women have attended evangelistic talks up and down the UK.

In any given group the ratio of Christians to non-Christians will vary, but a rough average would be half and half. In some areas there is only a handful of Christians, and large numbers of non-Christians. Where the local church has an evangelistic programme there has been less need for a group to be formed. This has meant that the majority of groups have come into being where there is no live church reaching out into the community. This has led to a problem in nurturing new Christians. For many years now, local Bible-study groups have come into being to help and encourage them. Many of these women have little if any Bible knowledge, and so new approaches have had to be made. (Some newly committed women have been really turned off by the know-alls, the super-intelligent and the super-spiritual.) In some areas small one-to-one or group studies for beginners have been formed, where no Bible knowledge is assumed and the atmosphere is relaxed and open. Initially interested through a lunch, many have joined small beginners' group Bible Studies and have become Christians in the following weeks.

Society is changing all the time, and any organisation aware of the societal trends constantly needs to listen to the voice of change, and adapt accordingly. CLDC has been changing constantly. Then we met in smart hotels, with white-gloved waiters and a large three-course lunch. Now we meet more informally. *Where* you live in Britain still makes for differences. In the North and in rural and provincial areas, lunch is still the main meal of the day. In London, the home counties, and in bigger cities, men and working women are still away for the whole day, and the evening meal is the social get-together.

Local pubs are often good places to eat; at Gerrards Cross the CV meets at ten am in the Jolly Farmer. Coffee is served, after which the speaker talks openly about Jesus. There is usually plenty of time for people to ask questions and to relate what they have heard to their own experience. Pub business is then resumed. Guests are free to stay on for a ploughman's lunch with Christian friends, and the conversation opportunities are extended informally in this delightful situation. As such venues have become more typical, the name of the organisation has had to change. With more and more groups having coffee and/ or ploughman's lunches, it seemed right to move to a more accurate title. 'Christian Viewpoint' has done much to put to rest the too exclusive image of the former CLDC.

Variety

If variety is the spice of life, CV has a rich flavour! Take Bournemouth for instance. Once a month you can turn up in the company of 500–600 other women to a delicious lunch served by attentive staff in the Brighton Pavilion. You will sit at a table for 12 and be well looked after by your own table hostess. Poole CV has fairly recently branched off from Bournemouth and runs two consecutive days of outreach events, using one speaker in two different venues to different audiences. You might sit in the premises of a restaurant, a sailing club, or a local community centre.

As entertaining at home has become more casual and food preparation less time-consuming—especially with the move away from large midday meals—more Christian women who have large enough homes to accommodate them are using their homes to reach women for Christ. A large number of groups for 30–60 women meet regularly on this basis. The food is simple and well presented, with an eye to the detail so much appreciated by women. There is a strong emphasis on caring friendships in a warm, relaxing atmosphere. The cost is minimal (£1–£1.50 almost everywhere). Every CV group member pays an annal subscription of £7, and receives the current lists and information and the magazine three times a year. The finances of the local group are autonomous, and vary widely. As Leigh-on-Sea, for example, where about 35–40 women come regularly to lunch, no charge at all is made for lunch. Their expenses for food and travel for the speaker have always been met by prayer and simply by placing a basket for gifts on the table.

In Greater Manchester, many new groups are forming, meeting mainly in the most suitable public or church halls. Fire regulations may limit numbers to 100 or 150, and many have waiting lists for tickets. The faith of the women who set out somewhat timidly to bring Christ to their friends has been enormously strengthened by specific answers to prayer regarding the availability of a specific building, the provision of necessary finance, and their own friends finding the Lord.

Ethne Mason, from a village in Kent, is married with two children aged 21 and 19. Writing in the Christian Viewpoint magazine, she says,

> I was brought up in a religious Welsh background. In spite of a happy marriage and family life, I was aware of a very big gap in my life. Various experiences and events set me thinking. I became quite seriously ill on several occasions. I thought about death a lot and what happens afterwards. It made me fearful and uncertain so I threw myself into lots of social work and tried to be 'good'. I realised we had lived a very materialistic life and when a friend commented that I had everything, I asked myself why wasn't I truly happy and satisfied.
>
> I believe at this point I was reaching out to God, and when I was invited by a friend to go to a local Christian Viewpoint

lunch with her to meet a Mr Max Sinclair, miraculously recovered from a near-fatal accident, I accepted immediately. I
was made so welcome, and was amazed at the way Max and the
others spoke of their love and faith in Christ. I had *never* heard
people talk like this before. Jesus seemed so real to them. For
the next two months, I thought of little else, but knew of no one
with whom I could share my thoughts. I started to read the
Living Bible (from the beginning) and other Christian books,
and couldn't wait to get to the next meeting to hear Audrey
Coleman and then Wendy Moynagh. The love of God, and the
sacrifice of Jesus for me became real. I understood for the first
time what life was really about. I gave my life to Him and knew I
was born again of the Spirit. I felt a tremendous joy and inner
peace and this has never left me, in spite of some ups and downs.

   Within six months, with the friend who had invited me in the
first place, we began our own group in our village. Our
numbers are not large, and consist mainly of churchgoing
people, but I want to introduce them to Jesus and hope to see
lives changed as mine was. 'Once I was blind, but now I can
see.' We are going on praying and believing for miracles.

Many church leaders support local CV groups, aware that
they offer new evangelical opportunities in a community
where the vast majority of people do not go to church.
Others look upon such parachurch activity as a threat to
existing women's work, and a few have been openly
antagonistic. In many areas, wives of clergymen have joined
local CV committees, at the same time keeping very strong
links with the church. Local Christian bookshops or book
agents almost always provide bookstalls for CV events, and
hundreds of books are bought by women hungry for truth
and spiritual reality. Short, punchy book reviews are a
regular part of many lunches.

   With numbers of working women growing in Britain, CV
committees are aiming to provide evening events which will
attract single and married career women. Many Scottish
groups (some affiliated to CV, others not) hold supper or
coffee evenings to which large numbers of working women
come.

In areas of high unemployment, for example the North East of England, the local problems and culture will demand a different approach. Lunchtime activity is in the minority, and morning events with a cup of coffee draw large numbers. One church in Leeds, for example, offers what it calls the Monday Break for women at home with children.

Whatever the nature of the CV outreach event, women come because they enjoy being with their friends, and it is the reality of the love of Christ demonstrated by the Christian neighbour that earths the talk by a speaker. Real needs of women are addressed by the speakers—the lonely housewife problem; the professional single woman's problems; marriage and relationship problems (rarely tackled by the local church, yet at least one in three women has marriage difficulties in British society); problems caused by illness, depression, death in the family, teenage rebellion and redundancy.

Well-known celebrities, such as Fiona Castle (wife of Roy) and Gerald Williams, guarantee a crowd. Any human-interest story with a clear testimony of how Christ has entered a person's situation gets a ready ear and a good response. Booklets to help those interested to become Christians are always available (funded by CV members) free of charge—*Start a New Life*, by David Watson, *Journey into Life*, by Norman Warren, or *Knowing God Personally*, by Campus Crusade.

Motivation

Women all over Britain, prompted by the Holy Spirit, are noticeably on the move to bring their friends to Christ. With many Christian and non-Christian women based at home during the day and the Church often silent in the face of their needs, Christian women are excited at taking Christ to their neighbours. Homes small and large are being offered to the Lord, and friends are being introduced to one another and the Lord. All sorts of gifts are being discovered and used—gifts of design in creating invitation cards; gifts of hospitality, friendship and encouragement; gifts of cooking, arranging welcoming flowers, as the reality of the living Christ is demonstrated and absorbed.

One disturbing factor urgently needs to be addressed. Across Britain, women are being won for Christ, but what about the husbands? So long as children continue to be born in Britain, a large proportion of married women will be home-based, and thus are more available to come out during the day. Are these women perhaps nearer the nitty-gritty issues of life and death than their husbands? Are they looking for the meaning to life which bypasses the more self-sufficient work-orientated male?

Whatever the answer to these questions, the thousands of women who are finding Christ and are married to non-Christian men are finding the going tough. Some are discouraged by unsympathetic husbands from attending church, reading the Bible and from meeting with Christian friends. Others struggle with the fact that loving Christ means not marrying non-Christian men in the first place, even though there are few eligible single Christian men in our churches. Some men are finding Christ, but it is a long-term, open-ended commitment in lifestyle and prayer for a great many women, both married and single. Marriage— under attack anyway in our permissive culture—takes on the added pressure of two often opposing concepts of the whole purpose and meaning of life. And singleness is often misunderstood as being permissiveness, or a selfish way to live, possibly even 'anti-family'.

So—should CV cease to exist? Not until Jesus Christ rescinds his command to go and make disciples! Should the women perhaps redouble prayer for men to reach men where they are—in the pubs, at the cricket clubs, at lunch-hour events in local business centres and working men's clubs? Could the men take a leaf out of the women's book, provide a milieu that is relaxed and unthreatening and address the needs of others with the presence and power of the living Lord? Why not?   *Helen Cooke*

Helen Cooke is founder and President of Christian View-point, previously known as the Christian Lunch and Dinner Club. Originally set up to reach professional women, it is now open to women generally and thriving throughout the UK. Helen is mother of three grown-up daughters and is married to Nigel, who is Director of International Films.

10. Women in Prison

In Great Britain there are approximately 2,000 women and girls imprisoned. Compared to the 45,000 men, this may not seem many, but this figure does not indicate the number of women who are suffering abuse and violence within the home, and the young girls who are abused sexually within families. Thus many are in prisons made of concrete and iron, others are in emotional prisons which sometimes are even harder to escape.

Like men in prison, many women are from broken homes and backgrounds of abuse. It is surprising the number who first got into trouble, not through seeking to do wrong, but through running away from a situation that was severely disadvantaged or violent.

I myself was born into a home where violence was normal. This led me to run away. The only places open were all-night cafes. Here I met prostitutes and drug addicts, and it wasn't long before I was offered some pills, which I was told would help me. I eventually ended up in a series of remand homes, and before long I was in Borstal. I also started taking drugs regularly and became a registered heroin addict. Yet another incident that was to mark my life happened when at 14 I was raped. Because I was a runaway there was nothing I could do to get help. As a result of this incident, I became a lesbian as this seemed to be the only way I could be safe from men.

Suffering

It is important for Christians to realise that many women in prison have suffered much abuse and sexual perversion of this kind. Of course some deserve to be imprisoned; but many I know are from backgrounds similar to mine who, through seeking to escape from hurt, emotional or physical, have ended up in trouble with the law. As Christians are becoming more aware of social needs, more and more are praying for those from such a background.

Prisons have been quite rightly described as 'hell holes', and women are affected differently from men by imprisonment, perhaps because (in most cases) of the intensity of their emotional make-up. Occult activities are often practised, and lesbianism is the norm for many. An atmosphere of tension and violence is common. All this obviously affects the different individuals as they enter prison life. If one is spiritually sensitive, one can sense the evil that pervades these places. It was through people praying for me and over a long period reaching out to me that I eventually became a Christian. There are now prayer groups specifically for prisons all over Great Britain and Southern Ireland. I know this is good, for the battle is first and foremost spiritual, and when people pray, things do start to happen. It is important for people to understand that if someone has been abused and hurt, it takes quite a while before she can trust anyone at all. Although many were praying for me, the time came when one person in particular came into my life.

Joan was a Christian who came regularly to see me when I lived in London. She brought soup and sandwiches every Sunday but more important—plenty of love. She didn't preach at us, but became our friend. This in some ways is where it all starts, becoming a friend. Jesus was known as a 'friend of publicans and sinners' and Joan was just like that.

It may take a long time before a person is able to understand the message of Jesus; in my case it was ten years before I responded. But it was through Joan's contact that I was able to know where to turn when the time came. Also there were those who prayed for me for years. They must have felt like giving up at times, but they didn't, and eventually their faithfulness and prayers paid off.

The next thing that happened was that a couple were willing to take me into their home. I was still injecting six ampules of physeptone (synthetic heroin) a day, as a registered addict. Even so, they were willing to take me. Now there was a place for me to go. Even then, in my case, it was a good two years before I eventually responded to Jesus and asked him into my life. The church I went to gradually reached out to me in love, and one of its members gave me a part-time job. It was very important for me to feel accepted in this way, though there were always Christians who didn't seem to know how to respond to me. Even today, I often feel an object to be looked at and sense the uneasiness in some Christians once they know of my past.

It is important that Christians should be able to listen to the stories of those who come from certain socially deprived backgrounds. Part of feeling accepted is knowing people understand you, and before true forgiveness can enter a woman's life, she has to feel free to share. In a society where sexual abuse in becoming more and more common, Christians need to be able to share Christ's love in a way that ministers even to the sordid incidents that are often in women's pasts. Freedom in Jesus, and knowing they are not only forgiven, but cleansed, are essential. A friend of mine who often ministers to women says to them, 'Once you have accepted Christ's forgiveness you are as a virgin in God's sight, no matter what you have done or had done to you sexually.' This is so true. Perhaps it is hard for some to understand the hurt and betrayal of trust that has marked many women's lives, as well as the problems that often result.

Emotional healing is a subject of concern among many branches of the Church today. Some people are however still wary of deliverance ministries, and others have been insensitive in the way they have used these in people's lives. However, I am convinced that the ministry of deliverance is essential to many who are in prison—both literally and spiritually—and who come from socially deprived backgrounds. It was only as I was healed from the past and set free from demonic influences that I was able to leave drugs, lesbianism, and all that went with them. I believe God wants more and more people who are willing to become the instruments of healing and deliverance to free people in these situations.

Guidelines for Reaching Out to Women in Prison

Where does one begin to help women in prison? First, make contact. Do not come with preconceived ideas or methods of evangelism, but come to befriend in the name of Jesus. Whether this takes place in a prison visiting room or in a cafe or club is irrelevant—your attitude is more important.

For some this may mean fresh training and new ways of ministering, but it is worthwhile. Though the world itself is anti-Christ, there are many people who are open to Jesus, if only Christians would have the patience, love and understanding to reach out sensitively in his name. Prison distorts and hardens a woman's personality, but God can 'straighten a person out'. This does take time. It doesn't usually happen overnight, and long-term support and care are necessary.

Be prepared to care for women (or one woman) long-term. I pulled my life together with God's help in the home provided for me. Both through people's love and commitment, and through individual encounters with Jesus, I was set free from the demonic influences in my life. This led—against all the odds—to my coming right away from a lifestyle that was killing me. I now have a life to lead as a Christian. This change in some ways was hardest of all.

Because of my background I felt people saw mine mainly as a sensational testimony, but as time passed, I found somewhere to live myself and started to get involved in a

YMCA coffee bar, which is a Christian based outreach. Here I had found a niche and a base. I was able to help and understand those from similar backgrounds to my own. I started to get letters from many people who had been in prison, suffered abuse, or were on drugs. God has been able to use my past positively. I am very aware that I am alive because of Jesus, and also that Jesus used people to reach out to me.

Prayer is the fundamental element in all outreach. First, Christians need to read about social problems so that they can pray for many who are imprisoned. Information from organisations already working in this area may lead to contact in visiting a prison, writing to a prisoner or supporting a discharged prisoner. However, you should realise that it is a long-term commitment; do not make contact with a person in prison if you are not willing to carry through the commitment to the end. Some start visiting or writing letters and then stop. This can be shattering, because yet again the prisoner faces rejection. So it is very important to count the cost of what you are getting involved in. Sometimes during the long-term contract, it may seem that everything is going wrong and that the person you are praying for—or in contact with—is getting worse rather than better. Be patient and continue praying.

Links with professional as well as Christian people are helpful; if you want contact with prisons in Great Britain write to the Prison Fellowship, which will seek to give you advice and guidance.

I emphasise—do not be shocked by anything you may hear. Women need to be able to talk about what has happened, and you should keep this information confidential. Love and healing need to be applied sensitively to the hurts. Be prepared for a satanic backlash as you get involved. Satan does not like people reaching into what he thinks is his area. You will draw attack, so put on the full armour of God outlined in Ephesians 6.

It is good that Christians seem to be growing more aware of women in prison. A friend of mine often says 'the people in the deepest need in our society often get the least amount of care from the body of Christ.' I feel this is true, but things are changing. I encourage you to reach out in Jesus' name with the support of like-minded Christians, and I know many like me will be helped by your prayers and love.

Anita Hydes with Tony Ralls

Anita Hydes is a voluntary worker at the YMCA in Sidmouth, where she is involved in counselling, evangelism and a wide letter-writing ministry. She speaks in prisons and schools on drugs education, a ministry which has grown from her own involvement in prison and the drug scene. Anita's full story can be read in the book Snatched From The Flames, *published by Marshall and Pickering, price £1.95. Also, if you would like to write to Anita she can be contacted at the YMCA, Mill St, Sidmouth, Devon, England.*

11. Reaching Young and IsolatedWomen

'What's good about being a girl?' 'What's bad about being a girl?' Over in the corner of the room, two groups of 13- to 16-year-old girls work together, identifying things from their own experience that they enjoyed or found difficult about being girls—girls growing up on a large council estate in an inner-city area.

As they came back into the centre of the room and shared experiences, I thought about their answers and about my own experiences as a girl. Were they that different? They enjoyed being with their friends, going out, having a laugh, talking, dressing up, clothes, music. They disliked periods, having to do more housework than their brothers; were afraid of walking home in the dark, being called names by boys, and being laughed at.

After the discussion was over, I asked them why they came to a girls' only 'night' in the youth club. Some said because they could do more when the boys weren't around. Others said they could be themselves more easily, whereas the boys would tell them they were silly. Others were afraid of the boys who came to the mixed nights in the youth club.

Why have girls' nights and girls-only 'work' become an important area of development in youth clubs around the country? Only twenty years ago the emphasis was on mixed clubs. Why have things changed? What is happening in the clubs that make girls want separate evenings? And how can the Gospel be communicated to girls and female youth effectively today?

Looking Back

The first recognition that those girls' needs were not being met in mixed clubs came in the late 1970s. Youth workers became aware that the male membership of youth clubs far outstripped the female membership and that the traditional programme—of sports, competitions, weekends away—was failing to attract more than a small percentage of girls. Often club workers were men. In time female helpers were asked to discover what the girls wanted to do. Although it appeared initially that all they wanted to do was sit and talk, some women youth workers felt that given space on their own, the girls would become more active. Clubs began to join together and organise girls' days and girls' weekends away when girls would try out activities that they normally watched the boys doing, eg, rock climbing, woodwork and motor-cycling. In addition, activities like self-defence, beauty care and jewellery-making were included, which the girls said they felt silly doing in front of boys. Time was set aside during girls' days and weekends for discussions. Most of the organisers were surprised how well they were attended and how much the girls participated. This led eventually to some of the clubs introducing girls' nights or times during the mixed clubs when girls had first choice of activities. When I started working in youth clubs six years ago, I had already spent three years training as a youth worker and two years working in mixed clubs, but I had applied for a job with particular emphasis on working with girls. My aim was to see how I could be involved in developing activities that would meet their need. I work in a large inner London Christian youth club which has been active now for over 80 years.

From meeting some of the girl ex-club members on the street, I have realised that they want to maintain contact with the club. Sometimes they come to my house; at other times we meet and go out for a drink. In this way I can keep in touch with them, encourage them to think about what they are doing with their lives, and be a support to them in times of difficulty. What does this mean in practice?

Shirley

I have known Shirley for six years (not her real name). She came into club with a group of ten girls about her age when she was 14. At first, I saw her as one of the quieter members of the group, which as a whole were often quite demanding. She was one of four children living in overcrowded accommodation and sharing a tiny room with a sister five years younger than herself. Her parents were quite strict, so she had to be home considerably earlier than the other girls. She was always ready to talk about school, boyfriends, or whatever concerned her. When she was 15, a group of her friends started coming to a fellowship meeting in the club. Afterwards many of them would meet together in a discussion group, sharing their fears, hopes and problems in relationships.

When Shirley was 16, she started drinking. She would turn up at the club, sit on the steps outside, or complain of headaches. One of us would go out and talk to her and give her some black coffee to enable her to sober up before she went home. When she left school, she would come to club and tell us all about her job in a large chain store and people with whom she worked. Unfortunately, she was soon laid off with many of the other school leavers who had started work that year. Unemployed, she spent time with her friends on the streets and got involved in smoking cannabis and experimenting with other drugs.

During that time she still came to the club and through a misunderstanding one night got into a fight with me which left me with a split lip. For a while, she drifted away but started coming to my home for a chat about once a fortnight, on Saturday mornings. As we talked, we discussed my Christian views and her own ideas about life. While she was interested to talk more about God, she couldn't commit herself actually to sit down and look at the Bible with me. Recently I asked her what she believed. She explained that she believed in God and that Jesus was God's Son, and that he forgave people their sins because he had died for them, but she didn't believe in life after death or that Jesus had risen from the dead. We discussed how much she had been influenced by meeting Christian leaders in the club. She admitted she had taken in more than she had realised, and although initially she thought that the Christian epilogue spots were boring, she had remembered quite a bit. She saw the Christians in the club as people with a different view of life from her own, but who had shown her what love and commitment really meant. She still wouldn't call herself a Christian, but felt she was 'getting there'.

Shirley's spiritual pilgrimage has taken six years from her first encounter with Christians. Along the way she has had times of crisis and has been helped through by those who have known her most closely. No one preached at her during those times, but they were available and cared. She is now asking more questions—aware that she will have people around her whom she can call upon when she needs.

Recently Shirley has also put me back in touch with one of her friends. This girl became more heavily involved in the drug scene, got addicted to heroin and gave birth to a baby which had to be weaned off drugs during the first week after her birth. Shirley asked me to call her, because she felt this girl was lonely and was likely to go back on drugs. Since contacting her, I have put her in touch with a group set up to support isolated young women, and she is spending time with the worker from that project learning about ways of looking after her baby and meeting other young women in similar situations. (The worker with this group is a Christian who brings her faith into her work, believing that the young women she is working with can be offered hope in what are often very hopeless circumstances: through friendship, listening, shared experiences, fun, and learning new skills.)

The Invisible and the Isolated

Married women and professional women can often be seen out shopping and going to and from work. Young mums often meet and talk outside the school gates or go to mother and toddler groups. Yet many girls once they have left school have few regular places where they can meet together. At school, they will have gone around in a group of four or five, but once they start work or stay at home un-employed, there is no longer the same common bond between them. Some have boyfriends, but for those who do not enjoy the disco, pubs, or student life, the transitional period into young adulthood is often a time of vulnerability and loneliness. Most girls have one or two friends with whom they shop or spend time in each other's houses. However, many feel that they are losing out, especially the unemployed. They see other girls enjoying themselves with more money while they are at home most nights watching TV.

It is among this group in particular (who are often 16 or 17 years old) that youth workers like myself and other volunteers could set up activity-based groups to bring isolated young women together. Such a group could meet on a fort-nightly basis to do things together such as swimming, going to a show, or getting involved in community projects such as decorating, gardening and shopping for the disabled.

Activity groups of this kind have been set up in different parts of the country to work with isolated young women. Often those who are contacted have been young women known to youth club leaders in the past, or known to careers services or health visitors. One young woman who is involved in a local project in London was at a boarding school for slow learners. She came home after leaving school and was unemployed for a year. Her life revolved around looking after her brother and sister and visiting elderly relatives. She has gradually been drawn into the project. Someone has gone shopping with her to help her choose clothes (she gets confused about money), someone else is helping her to find a job—all ways of sharing God's love with a person who feels 'on the outside'.

Another young woman involved with the project is 20 and has a three-year-old child. Although she had been to mothers and toddlers' groups, she wanted to do more than just chat over coffee, but she did not have the confidence to join an adult education class. In a small group of four at the project, she learnt silk-screen printing on material, and how to make up her own designs and clothes. Through this friendship with the workers at the project she has talked often about what she believes in. At the moment, she is thinking about whether or not to have her child christened (she understands now why the local vicar would not christen the child because she did not go to church), and if she did, what that would mean. She also wants her child to go to a church school so that she gets a Christian education and Christian influence from the teachers. She has been to a carol service; the next step might be to take her to a family service.

For so many people, going to church is an alien and even nerve-racking experience. One youth worker I know talked with some women in a tenants' association recently about church involvement. He soon realised that the women wanted to talk about God but wouldn't go to church. This is not uncommon. So he invited a few of them around to his house to the Good Friday meal—just soup and bread by candlelight. There they talked freely about the meaning of Easter in a way which was personal and appropriate.

Ways of Getting Involved

Working in a Youth Club

I remember the first time I went into a local authority youth club: I was 'on placement' as part of my course, and was scared stiff about what I might find. I was worried that I wouldn't know what to say or do. I stood at the door and saw the kids smoking, sitting around and generally not doing much. The pool and table-tennis tables were empty. In the corner, an older lady stood chatting with some girls, a man went round trying to get others to go on a trip. It all seemed so different from my own experience from being in a church youth club where we all wanted to do things all the time, arrange meetings ourselves and were generally more enthusiastic.

Over the next few weeks, I realised that the young people going to club here nevertheless went for almost the same reasons as I had. They wanted to get out of their homes, to a place where they could be with friends and away from their parents. How was I to get involved? It looked as if the girls just needed someone to open up the place, make sure they didn't set it on fire, leave them to it, and then put off the lights and lock up at the end of the evening. I found out that they needed someone to serve in the sweet shop, but how was I going to form relationships with the ones in the corner? I enjoyed doing a lot of different activities in my own spare time. Could I ever use these to help these young women?

Nine years later, having spent hours watching other new volunteers come in wondering how they fit in, I still remember my own first experiences.

The volunteers come in to lend a hand, teach jewellery-making, take kids canoeing and engage in a whole host of other activities. For some their main reason in helping is to build up a relationship with the young people so that they can share their faith with them. This has to be done in a way that is appropriate to those who come, and mistakes are made by over-enthusiastic new volunteers.

On one occasion club members had asked some volunteers why they went to church. One volunteer explained how she had found a relationship with God and went to church to spend more time with him. One of the girls took this up and said, 'It can't be much of a relationship if it only lasts one hour a week'. The volunteer was hurt by this remark and wondered where she had gone wrong.

So much of being with young people is about identifying with them—'being part of the furniture'. It is important that the girls themselves are motivated to plan their own agenda. Leaders and helpers may well be invited for suggestions and comments when ideas have run out. If a leader has a particular hobby, girls in club may well respond to it, asking the leader questions about their own life outside the club.

'Doesn't your husband mind you being here when he knows you get sworn at?' 'My Dad won't let my Mum come here!' 'Why don't you sleep with your boyfriend?' 'Why won't you buy nicked goods?' 'Did you ever have to be in at 10 o'clock?' 'Why do you work here for nothing?' These are the kind of questions club members ask. As relationships deepen, opportunities come to talk about life's attitudes, problems and faith.

One of the mistakes some youth workers make is to assume that the young person's main interest in club is getting to know them. They feel hurt if they are ignored, and they often give up. However, by staying there even when ignored or verbally abused, at times they are able to talk about what is important in their own lives, provided they are prepared to show an interest in learning about the girls' lives and value their experiences as well.

Many clubs are short of leaders, particularly female leaders, who are prepared to spend the time coming into club while relationships form over the first few months. All sorts of adults help in youth clubs. You don't have to be good at sport or craft, though if you have a hobby it could be used to teach young people a new skill. Provided you are interested in meeting young women, prepared to listen and willing to join in what's going on, anyone can help. The leaders of the girls' nights at my club in London come from a variety of backgrounds. One is a stockbroker who enjoys rowing and weight training. Another works as a packer in a tee-shirt factory. She is local, can drive, and knows a lot about what is going on in the area. Another woman works with computers and enjoys getting out and about. Between them they run activities for about 30 young women aged 14–28. In the first six months these have included making a video, weight training, self-defence (following a manual on the subject!), going for a sauna, going to the theatre, carol singing, going riding, sailing, or on a night walk. Jewellery-making while discussing health and local politics has also been part of the programme. None of the women would describe themselves as 'skilled youth workers'. They simply join in and learn with the girls. As a result, one girl has visited a leader's home to do some homework, and another met up with one of the leaders to go to a fashion show. One leader discovered that one of the girls could not read well and has offered to go to her house and help her. In the 'Good News' spots each night in the club, we have talked about women in the Bible, looking at different characters each night. Clubs like ours welcome offers from people to come and do short courses such as drama, beauty care, or woodwork. Other adults could simply come in one evening to share experiences of what it means—for example—to be a one-parent family, or how to make Christmas decorations.

Most people who volunteer to work in a club enjoy the activities as much as the young women they meet. They appreciate learning about young people's experience and come to realise that sharing in this way can sometimes lead them to give advice and support to individuals that they remember for the rest of their lives.

Encouraging Young Women in Church to Attend Non-church Youth Clubs

When I was 14, I started going to a church youth fellowship, and for the next four years most of my weekends were taken up with the activities of the group. With 40 to 50 members and a 'social' every Saturday there was no need for me to spend time with non-Christians, particularly as at school there were a large number of Christians in my class.

By contrast, my sister attended a local authority youth club. My evangelical parents worried about the sort of influences she would encounter there, but she enjoyed being away from our Christian family and needed the space to discover her own interests. Over the years she went on to the youth club members' committee and helped organised fund-raising events and holidays.

Ten years later, we are both involved in church life. Yet had our parents insisted that my sister went to the same church youth club as I did, she might not have come to Christian commitment, feeling perhaps she was not allowed the time or space to discover who she was in her own way.

Each young woman is different, but it is important to allow them to find faith in their own time. Ideally, it is good to encourage those (who can) to go to a church youth club for Christian support, but to develop friendships with girls at school who would be put off by going to a church club.

At present, there are four Christian girls coming to the girls' night in the club where I work. They all go to the church youth club on Sunday nights but come to our club on girls' night and help as leaders in the junior youth club. The other girls know they are Christians and sometimes comment on the fact that they don't swear or smoke. However, because the girls come with their non-Christian school friends (they all go to different schools), they are not an exclusive Christian group. Over the last six months they have invited four of the other girls to the church group, two of whom now come regularly. One has since become a Christian and is to be confirmed this year. They have shown their friends that as Christians they can enjoy life but at the same time are different.

So often Christian parents are afraid that their children will be drawn away from church if they get involved in non-Christian activities. Yet young people from churches can become 'salt' in an open youth club, provided they have the support and prayers of their churches behind them.

Providing Open House for Your Children's Friends or Teenagers You Know

Many homes or flats are so small these days that young people feel they have nowhere to go and sit with their friends. Consequently they go out and meet at the chip shop or McDonalds or stand in crowds on street corners. Yet often they just want a room to sit in where they can talk. Jane, mother of Lisa, a girl I knew from the club, was a strong Christian. Jane would often encourage Lisa to bring her friends in for cups of coffee. They lived in a small flat with a small kitchen and living room. Yet Jane would rather have five teenagers crowded in the kitchen smoking, than worry about them being on the streets. She didn't condemn what they talked about or tell them to stop smoking. She just gave them a place to sit. Years later one of Lisa's friends still talks about how Jane listened to them and had them so freely in her home.

Too many parents don't want their homes dirtied, or feel that their home isn't good enough to encourage their children's friends to come in. However, by being prepared to be put out a little, you may well be the adult who gives a few young people somewhere where they can be themselves outside their own homes. They might well open up to you once trust is established, share their ideas and problems and be open, too, to listen to yours. At the same time they might just need to be left on their own (perhaps to babysit for a small sum?) while you go next door.

Single women in particular may feel they can offer their flat for an evening a week for the young people to come round after church, or to come in and do their homework during weekdays.

A couple of girls have come to help me paint my house. Their parents didn't trust them at home with the paintbrush, but the fact that we can get messy together and then sit and talk over coffee has given real opportunities for the relationships to deepen, including talking quite openly about my faith with them and involvement in church.

There are all kinds of ways of helping girls and younger women by showing you care and bringing Christ's love to them, whatever situation they are in. I have discovered that the Gospel isn't just what you say—it's being available, ready to be ignored, abused, but believing and knowing that it is not in vain.

Alison Jones

Alison Jones trained as a youth worker in Birmingham, worked for two years in Belfast and seven years at the Cambridge University Mission in Bermondsey, London. She is now job-sharing as Community Worker at Bede House community project, and has had long-term experience working with girls and younger women.

12. Women and Fitness

Christians rightly concern themselves with spiritual growth and health. Often, however, those attracted to Christian friends can't identify with something that at first seems abstract to them. Instead, they may gravitate towards groups of Christian women who can offer them something at once familiar and useful—fitness. With today's emphasis on health and diet, exercise and wholefood cooking, fitness groups provide a natural avenue for outreach.

It was the challenge of Christ—to be involved in the lives of those around us—that prompted an ad hoc group of women (including myself) to start praying and caring for the needs of neighbours and friends. We started out in a general way, not entirely sure of our direction. Within the security of a comfortable lounge, we faced issues like cancer, self-defence, the breaking up of the family unit, abortion, child abuse, teenage problems and depression. A local doctor, a mastectomy aftercare consultant, a policeman and a fireman were among those willing to participate and discuss in practical ways a workable faith within these crucial concerns. Interspersed between meetings on these major issues were demonstration evenings on microwave cooking, leather craft, pottery, computers, flower arranging and hairdressing. These created a relaxed atmosphere for sharing our experiences and the reality of a relationship with Jesus. This in turn led on to strong friendships and a deeper sharing of the implications of Christian commitment. Local shops were very willing to introduce their goods by inviting our group to visit their premises, and clothing traders arranged an evening of fashion shows. Interest in swim and leisure wear, shoes, Scottish knitwear, dress fashions, toys, cheese and meat was encouraged by displays with opportunity for reduced cash purchasing. Visits to a local hair salon, a furrier, a garden centre, a shoe shop, all helped deepen our relationships and introduced our friends to local facilities as well as forging friendships between our church and local small businesses.

Friends and Neighbours

Our increased awareness of the local community showed us the need to involve all ages, on occasions both sexes, and certainly singles as well as marrieds. 'Friends and Neighbours' became an all embracing title for a mushrooming of activities that had their source in Jesus' command to 'go'. When we go, he accompanies us with his unique gift of communication flowing through our different personalities, to a neighbourhood of characters coloured by a God of infinite variety. A weekly Mother and Toddler group and more recently a bi-weekly nurture group became obvious 'next steps' as we forged relationships, and these have become a recognised part of our church programme. As friends were introduced to family services, outreach lunches, coffee mornings, and Sunday School, the prayers of the original planning group were for more regular in-depth contact with the neighbourhood so that those who were introduced to Jesus became committed to him for life.

Just two years after the original monthly 'Friends and Neighbours' started, a direct answer to these prayers came from the group itself. We had enjoyed a fun evening introducing Keep Fit for all ages and abilities. Questions and suggestions had come thick and fast, resulting in a strong request for a weekly class. Not recognising the significance of this, I came up with my fair share of excuses to avoid starting this form of outreach—lack of time, facilities, and understanding from other Christians of our real vision for commencing such an activity. None of these excuses held water. The one word common to them all reflected my lack of confidence in a God who loves to take our flimsy abilities, and multiply them beyond our wildest dreams for the extension of his Kingdom.

Ruth, one of the originators of our group, would not let the request for a weekly Keep Fit be forgotten. As I battled with the problem of time and willingness, she kept praying and prodding! With a back problem that had laid her flat for six months, Ruth knew her limitations and wasn't sure at first whether exercise was even possible for her. Six years later, through wise medical advice and gradually increased exercise, Ruth's back is much stronger and her presence in the group remains a source of encouragement to all, especially those with back problems!

If our initial outreach had not been rooted in prayer, and if the resulting activities had not driven us back to our dependence on God time and time again, our next step would have fizzled out like a damp firework. Too many of our selfish efforts became smouldering memories, but God had other plans. Having prayed for several months individually and collectively, we approached our church leaders and asked their advice on including a Keep Fit activity in the church programme. After we presented our case, there was a thoughtful silence. I am so thankful for leaders who took time to examine our motives and aims prayerfully, who entered into some of our excitement over this new project. Obviously they could not be sure of the outcome, but they were willing to back us up.

Keeping Fit

The youth centre at the rear of our church was put at our disposal for one night a week. As I prepared for that first nerve-racking, limb aching evening, I could only thank God for his unseen hand on my life 20 years before, when as a teenager I had gone to college at Eastbourne to specialise in Physical Education. The endless round of lectures on Anatomy, Physiology, Psychology and Education had been a grind. I had anticipated plenty of outdoor activity and competitive challenge, but now the all-round training could be channelled into presenting a relaxed, safe, and enjoyable approach to Keep Fit.

The gigantic wave of Western interest in physical fitness has gathered momentum, but it often leaves people in its wake disheartened and breathless—inadequate enthusiasts who can't live up to the 'body beautiful' image. The influence of immaculate advertising, fantasy soap operas, spectacular fashion and a sport-orientated society drags many people into strenuous exercise routines, impossible dieting, and plummeting depression. A sense of inadequacy prevents them from enjoying even simple leisure activities. For us to add another event to accentuate weaknesses and draw attention to failings was unwise, but God's word in all respects is incredibly practical. In my preparation for the first Keep Fit evening I was encouraged to read of the complete fitness of Jesus in Luke 2:52.

'Jesus grew in wisdom and stature, and in favour with God and men'. He knew about a developing fourfold fitness: physical, mental, spiritual, and social, which are all closely-related. We asked for his wisdom and approach to a fitness that would build people up, not knock them down; encourage rather than discourage; open them up to his potential rather than close them in to their own inadequacy; and which could help them enjoy the life that Jesus speaks of in John 10:10 'I have come that they may have life and have it to the full!'

Relaxing Together

Our aim on that first evening was to put our friends at ease. It was helpful to have a nucleus of people of different abilities and ages who were willing to start wherever they were, and if necessary to make fools of themselves. We found this to be an effective icebreaker. In retrospect, I see that it would have helped the group if we had met regularly not only in prayer, but also for exercising together, in learning to relax and laugh. Laughing is one of the most important exercises, physically, mentally and spiritually. To be at ease with ourselves and comfortable with the way God has made us opens wide a door to our full potential.

I worked long and hard in the early days on sequences of exercises for every area of the body, so that the movement matched the music. (Many of these are included in my two 'Fit for Life' cassettes produced by Word UK.) We checked the practicalities of insurance, and any licence fees that might have to be paid for the public performances of sound recordings. Selecting the right music was important, and improvisation helpful when members of the group brought along favourite cassettes. Their confidence grew as their own music was introduced. With such a wide variety of music today, we interspersed a wealth of different rhythms throughout the evening to prevent boredom. The thought-provoking words of some songs often led to questions and discussions over 'feet up' and coffee afterwards. The evening gradually developed into a vital oasis, very different from set preaching and epilogues. People talked about their own problems, and we took time to answer questions that arose from the other 'Friends and Neighbours' activities or from church services.

With all new ventures the novelty eventually wears off. This was particularly so in Keep Fit; people's spirits flagged, as well as general interest. I am thankful that through my involvement in this project and through God's discipline, I have discovered his renewing power in a practical way and the ability to keep going. The combination of music, movement and company has a reviving, soothing effect that God uses to deepen relationships, lift the spirit and remove the masks we so often hide behind. As in everything, stick-ability is essential. Deeper involvement in the health and well-being of our friends adds excitement to the mundane preparation and exhaustion of such an evening.

Fit for Life

A constant challenge after six years of Keep Fit outreach is the balance of preparation and participation. If we spend one hour in physical exercise plus an hour in preparation, we need to spend at least an equal amount of time, if not more, in the spiritual exercises of prayer and sharing our faith with those who join us. If we ask God to help us find time, we will always find it. He is the origin of invention and ingenuity, and this is what we need in controlling our time. We must not neglect uninterrupted, concentrated times of prayer, but God has given us many creative ideas, which keep us alert and exercised in prayer! Here are a few:

1. Small group prayer and exercise session.
2. Prayer as we prepare the room.
3. Back-up prayer team as the session is in full flight!
4. Silent prayer as we exercise.
5. Each Christian being responsible to pray and care for a set number of the group.

Many members of churches are willing to be part of a back-up prayer team. Although not vitally interested in Keep Fit, they are concerned for the spiritual wholeness that comes from introducing people to Jesus. We live in a world acutely aware of the physical body. We exercise it, feed it, pamper it, clothe it, paint it, measure it, weigh it, massage it, sun it, exploit it, sell it, and then eventually—we leave it! As I meet women all over the British Isles, I am seeing a growing number really enjoying this temporary body of ours. This enjoyment is not dependent on a sylph-like figure or athletic ability. It is in the discovery that God accepts us as we are, from the pensioner who described herself triumphantly as 'very well endowed' to little Clare on the cover of my second 'Fit for Life' cassette, very active in a wheelchair.

These women are accepting themselves as God accepts them, and as a result are facing up to the defects and disabilities that so often limit us. God has the habit of taking our weaknesses if we give them to him, and using them for his glory and for our benefit.

Acceptance is crucial as we welcome people to Keep Fit. Total acceptance is a crying need in all of us. If our friends and neighbours have not experienced God's acceptance, they can start tasting it as we welcome and love them. Our relationship with God can deeply affect our treatment and love of others. Taking the exercise as far as is comfortable for our structure and ability is what we consider 'success'. Whatever their shape or size, we aim to welcome the women who come to us and help them to accept themselves. With this unthreatening approach many find they are capable of far more than they realised, and are a lot happier to stop and watch if it is unwise to continue. We avoid too much emphasis on dieting and weight and find that a healthy awareness of the correct use and care of the body grows naturally from coming to terms with ourselves.

Qualifications are a tremendous help in embarking on this type of outreach, and the safety side of all physical activity is important. The Keep Fit Association offers courses of training. Meanwhile physiotherapists, remedial gymnasts, physical educationalists, nurses or doctors in your church and in your area can be encouraged to be involved, either practically or in an advisory capacity. Many churches find that when this form of outreach is backed up by prayer, God provides the right people to share in it. This should always include those with different strengths and shapes, as well as the more experienced and qualified.

A cross-section of abilities is visible proof that everyone in the group is included. This is essential not only for the group, but for God's Family as a whole. Everyone is acceptable, whatever age, ability or appearance. The impact is increased when people of varying abilities feel they can join me in leading the exercises. The sense of foolishness soon disappears when we see the intense concentration in the faces of those following the exercises. The attention is not focused on us but on the exercise we are attempting to execute. The mistakes we make put people at ease. The most memorable and companionable times are when we collapse in a heap and laugh! The release is tremendous.

Outreach

Our initial outreach was church-based, but with increased leisure time and improved sports facilities nationwide there are growing opportunities in reaching whole communities with united church efforts. I remember a visit to Northern Ireland where a comparatively small group of women had stepped out in faith and packed out a massive leisure centre and a neighbouring sports complex with friends and neighbours. Their Keep Fit mornings were followed by a light lunch and a spontaneous, effective opportunity to talk about our relationships. I returned to Christchurch (Bournemouth) with fresh vision for a developing area close by, where the building of a new Sports Centre is planned. Swindon churches also pack their local sports centre monthly with hundreds of youngsters contacted through their youth groups. In a neutral venue, with use of all the facilities, teenagers of all abilities can alternate from badminton to swimming, squash to snooker. One cold night in January, I was invited to include two sessions of pop-mobility to their already strenuous evening. The reception to my spiritual sharing afterwards in a packed snooker room was, I'm sure, largely due to the town's united prayer backing.

The excitement in everything God initiates is seeing him use the most unlikely people to continue and enrich his work. Let us never underestimate what God can do through our lives and the situations through which we pass.

Keep Fit has enabled us to share deeply in each other's problems. Recently we all went through sadness following the sudden death of Ruth's husband, John. Ruth knew she could come through her grief and be accepted as she was. The music—so often a spring to our emotions—helped her to release her sorrow. Its impact, shared with those who don't yet know God personally, has been powerful, and Ruth is having endless opportunities to tell the reason for her peace and hope. Others who have lost people close to them feel a security with us, as the group has united in this experience.

February 14th for some is a romantic night out or a time to puzzle over intriguing mystery cards. For Jenny it was heartache. The night before, her husband had left her with their two boys. To miss Keep Fit did not enter her head on that Valentine's Day. She needed to let off steam and un-burden her confused mind. Having grown up on a farm, Jenny is extremely strong, and her lithe figure makes her expert in demonstration. Neither of us felt like leading on that dark, cold night, but Keep Fit provides a unique oppor-tunity to share hard as well as happy times.

Sally has joined us more recently. Her relationship with her husband Bob and a family of boys is admired by all who come into contact with them. Bob has his own business and is a very gifted organiser. When Sally accepted Jesus into her life, she found an added dimension to her already full and enjoyable existence.

'I'm not without my problems,' she says, 'but I am begin-ning to understand what real life is all about!'

These three stories, similar to many others, are all un-finished, because our involvement through outreach in Keep Fit goes on. It does not stop when a friend accepts Christ. Neither does our acceptance of someone grind to an embarrassing halt when they reject our faith. We have en-couraged an honesty that needs to be respected. Out of this refreshing frankness our nurture group was born (a parallel fitness group for our spiritual lives). Those who have ques-tions about God and what the Bible has to say are joined by new Christians. Using the Good News Bible for easy reference and reading, we study a wide variety of subjects including prayer, guidance, doubt, fear and assurance. Small group participation encourages discussion, response and prayer. More established Christians learn so much from the fresh enthusiasm of new Christians, and those still searching have plenty of opportunity to state their views and ask questions. The fun approach of the physical fitness spills over into these times of spiritual growth. We all thoroughly enjoy these bi-weekly evenings!

By writing this chapter, I have been able to praise God for the past, to increase my prayers for the present, and to raise my expectation for the future. One thing we are looking forward to is a few days away in the heart of the Dorset countryside. The barn dance we will enjoy then is a natural introduction for the Friends and Neighbours contacts to our church family. The elders and deacons put on aprons to cook for the barbecue, join in the dancing, and welcome the husbands introduced at these evenings. Some of the youth club direct the traffic, arrange the lighting and this year introduce their music group.

We are catering for 150, around 50 per cent of whom have not yet experienced the rebirth that comes when Jesus enters our lives through his Holy Spirit.

Keep Fit has been a God-given 'short cut' into the hearts and lives of many families. God has given us his confidence that 'he who began a good work in you will carry it on to completion until the day of Christ Jesus! (Phil 1:6).

Suggestions for Meetings

1. Healthy approach to diet, with a visit from local dietician.
2. Recipe and taste evening for sharing wholesome balanced foods.
3. Book local sports centre or village hall for sport outreach.
4. Health and fitness talks with local doctor.

5. Self-defence courses or single evening.
6. Keep fit with Weight-Watcher meals to follow.
7. Leisure and sportswear fashion show.
8. Local fun run to support Christian work or local immediate need.
9. Join local health and exercise club to reach into community.
10. Family swimming event.
11. Rambling club.
12. Medical evenings on subjects such as depression, heart problems, stress, anorexia.

Sue Barnett

Sue Barnett works for the Saltmine Trust, an evangelistic charitable trust which works extensively in the UK on missions, in schools and wherever there is the chance to preach the gospel. She is author of Fit for a King *(Kingsway) and married to Doug. They have two children.*

13. West Indian Women

Every race has its own valuable contribution to make to the community in which it finds itself. West Indian women in Britain are no exception. It has long been recognised that 'variety is the spice of life', yet as a minority group their cultural contribution is at best often misunderstood, and at worst ignored.

In this chapter I will attempt to open a window on West Indian women; try to give a realistic view to other women who may be genuinely trying to reach these women to understand their cultures, customs and general characteristics; and show West Indian women themselves how they can communicate the Good News of the Gospel to other West Indians and to others from different cultural backgrounds.

West Indian Women in Britain Today

It is difficult to obtain statistics solely on West Indian women apart from their families, but of the total West Indian population in Britain today the majority are women. The first influx of West Indian women arrived in the United Kingdom in the early fifties from the Caribbean (mostly from Jamaica). They came to join their husbands or fiancés, some to seek employment, some to further their education and training, but in all came seeking a better way of life.

Following the first arrivals, another group came in the

sixties, this time mainly from the Eastern Caribbean and
Guyana.

Difficulties of Adapting to White British Culture

Much credit should be given to West Indian women living in
the United Kingdom for their God-given resilience and
strength. Often this did not come directly from a personal
experience with the Living God; although most West Indians
are God-conscious, due to the basic teachings they received
about God from parents and grandparents, and in Sunday
Schools.

West Indians in general believe that Britain is the land of
Hope and Glory, and Mother of the Free; however, these
myths soon vanish on arrival. Newcomers find themselves
having to cope with drastic climatic changes for which they
are totally unprepared. Often they arrive in the winter in
summer dresses, with no coats or winter woollies. They may
be greeted with an unfriendly welcome from neighbours, or
find that living accommodation is impossible to obtain, as
advertisements read 'No Blacks'; employment is scarce—
often if a black person turns up to answer an advert, the
vacancy no longer exists; they discover that there is no
acceptance in the established churches. These are only
some of the difficulties that present extreme hardship.

Racial Barriers and the Good News

I arrived here as a young West Indian woman in May 1954.
Those were bleak, damp, wintry days when the sun hardly
appeared until late June or early July. Mist and fog
frequently covered most of the sky. It was then that I started
to appreciate the sunshine I had left behind in Jamaica. I
came as a trainee nurse into the secure surroundings of
Netherne Hospital, Surrey. The Matron, a lovely Scots lady,
made me feel very welcome and asked me to look on
Netherne as my home. It was a lovely gesture. Hence my
first experiences were completely different from those of

most new arrivals, yet that did not alter the fact that I was a West Indian woman in Britain, far from my real home.

I managed to deal with the day-to-day situations as they arose, as deep within me was the conscious realisation that Jesus had brought me here, and that he could keep me here. Proverbs 3:6 says 'In all your ways acknowledge him'. John 8:12 also came alive for me, and I clung to these precious words as I looked around for other Christians.

On the second day after my arrival in Britain, as I stood in the hospital corridor waiting to be interviewed by the matron, I noticed a young woman coming towards me. She seemed composed and happy. We exchanged 'hellos' and had a brief chat. I then discovered she was another Jamaican like myself. Later I learned she was a religious person without a real relationship with Christ, and that her name was Muriel.

Following my first meeting with Muriel, I was invited a few days later to the Nurses' Christian Fellowship. This was presided over by the hospital chaplain for the benefit of the Protestant nurses. Muriel was there as well.

After the formal business of the meeting, the Chairman asked me if I would sing one of our folk songs. I declined to do so as I have never practised folk singing, nor was I a soloist, but I offered to sing a sacred or religious song, as I was sure the Lord would help me in this. That night I sang 'As I travel through this pilgrim land there is a Friend who walks with me, Leads me safely through the sinking sand, He is the Christ of Calvary'. At the end of the meeting, an English nurse asked me when I applied to come to England. She then told me that this was about the same time she had prayed to God to send another Christian to join her. From then on, we became friends and met regularly in each other's rooms for prayer. At times, there were as many as six of us and Muriel started coming as well. Our friendship deepened, and we began sharing the same interests. I am happy to say I have had the joy of seeing her life changed by the power of God, from just a nominal churchgoer, to a radiant, committed Christian. Today, along with her family, she has touched myriads of other lives. With God, nothing is impossible, not even for West Indian women living in the United Kingdom.

These women know that once they are here in Britain, life is not a 'bed of roses', nor the paradise they dreamed about. Yet they are willing to stick with the hardships and difficulties they face, for one thing is certain—that they are seeking a better way of life for themselves and their children. But how do they cope and manage to succeed in this new society?

I will re-emphasize here that their *God-fearing* nature is the foundation on which many of their enduring qualities rest. West Indian women are ambitious, independent, industrious, hard working, loving and caring. They are friendly and helpful to each other. Most families are very close, and even seem inseparable at times. Their visits to each other are frequent and spontaneous; invitations are not thought necessary.

There are different customs and cultures within each ethnic group, and each seeks to maintain their cultural identity. However, almost all West Indian women are assertive. They take on the running of the home and will seek out their children's welfare in education and all that concerns them. Some see difficulty as a challenge to their capabilities and will go all out to master the situation rather than sitting back helplessly. For example, in broken marriages, some will use their initiative to provide a future for themselves and their children by finding employment.

Some of the earlier West Indian women were at a great disadvantage educationally, owing to the size of the families from which they came. An elder sister may have had to help at home with the care of smaller brothers and sisters, especially where the mother was ill, or where there were other misfortunes in the family. This was always at the expense of her own schooling, which meant in some cases that she might barely be able to read.

Times have changed, and we have come a long way since those days, but most women still abide by the principles they were taught to respect their elders and never contradict what they say rightly or wrongly. To be seen to do so would be 'asking for trouble'.

Back in the West Indies, there is not much scope outside the home for the average woman. Women are expected to do their domestic chores and fulfil the wife and mother role, as the case may be, but here in the United Kingdom, the same women have greater opportunity to receive formal education. They can compete in the world and earn their own money, often for the first time. Many seek to learn other skills at evening or night classes eg typing, dressmaking, self-defence and baking. They try to do these things in addition to their usual duties in the home. In traditional West Indian families men are not domesticated. They have been accustomed to being waited on by their womenfolk. Here in Britain the change in lifestyle calls for adjustment and adaptation by the men. When this is not forthcoming, increased strain and tension often result.

West Indian women are generally in no hurry to see their children leave home before they are ready to do so. The fact that West Indian girls remain at home longer than other girls of the same age in the UK does not make them less vulnerable to sexual harrassment than others are. In fact the problem is more pronounced within the home, particularly between step-fathers and step-daughters. Sound Christian teaching on biblical principles about sex and the sanctity of marriage remains really important and helps to create a healthy atmosphere for harmonious living, irrespective of race. Here the Church has a vast responsibility which needs to be faced—that of providing a safe place where their young women can talk about personal worries in confidence.

Problems for West Indian Girls

West Indian girls are faced with enormous challenges in society. At times, parents are not fully aware of the hurdles they must cross before they can find their real identity. There is the racial hurdle which reminds them daily that as blacks, they are a minority in a predominantly white society. They do not naturally belong, in spite of the fact that they were born here. Next is the cultural hurdle, where they are expected to live in two worlds at the same time. In Christian homes, teenage hostility towards West Indian custom and culture is suppressed to a degree, but in non-Christian homes open defiance and rebellion result, especially during the adolescent stage.

The next hurdle lies in the nature of the immigrant population in the areas where these girls live, and the ethnic mix of the schools and churches which they attend. Examples of this can be seen in the lives of three West Indian girls: Donna, Sandra and Claudette. They are all in their early twenties and were born in England. Donna, my daughter, lives and went to school in Norbury, a suburban area of London. Here, the ethnic population was quite small in the school. She attended the local Baptist church which was predominantly white, and went through Sunday School and Girls' Brigade. She'd become a Christian in one of their youth camps at the age of 16. She is now a youth leader with another white girl. Although she has had a traditional West Indian upbringing, due to the nature of her community, Donna finds it difficult to relate to some of the issues faced by other black girls.

Sandra lives in Brixton, a well-known inner-city area, and went to school just outside central Brixton. Her church is in the same area, which has a high ethnic population. This young woman describes herself as having suffered psychologically in some way, leaving her with an inferiority complex, although she knows that she is not inferior. She feels this has been brought about by peer pressure and pressure from society, where people 'talk down' to her. Through her relationship with the Lord, she has gained a sense of self-worth, but feels strongly that more help should come from the Church. The Church should be supplying people who are available and willing to listen to the cries of young black people calling for help.

Claudette also lives in Brixton. She went to the same school and goes to the same church as her friend Sandra. She is also from a typical West Indian background where a strong influence was maintained at home on traditional values, only loosened gradually as she approached her late teens. Rules such as attending church and Sunday School regularly were obligatory. Evenings out with girlfriends were heavily monitored to protect her reputation.

Friendship between the sexes at an early age is not permitted, as young West Indians are encouraged to study first to achieve the necessary qualifications, before thinking seriously about the opposite sex. This was very hard to take when Claudette's white peers had freedom in these areas from a much earlier age. Claudette said she felt pressured, constantly in a tug of war between the two cultures. As she grew older, she felt she could discuss topical issues, such as sex before marriage, abortion or rape more freely. Even so, she felt this new freedom was a real threat, and took great care not to betray the new boundaries of parental trust.

A Place to Talk

Traditionally, the church has lacked places where young West Indian women can talk. I feel the time has come for trained counsellors to be provided, and suitable areas where young people can meet; it should be made known that this facility is available to them. This would be not only for those young people who are already associated with the Church, but also for those who have no church contact. Claudette pointed out that where there is a strong mother/daughter relationship, there is less need for in-depth counselling; nevertheless fellowship with one another is top priority.

Building Friendship and Communicating the Gospel

Through the experiences of West Indian women, it can be seen that faith in the Living God has been their sustaining factor. Let us look at the following steps, which, if carefully followed, will lead to success in our witness.

1. **Faith in God** will work for all who have a personal relationship with him, irrespective of race or nationality as long as your desire is to glorify him.
2. **Prayer** is a very important ingredient to be mixed with faith. Whatever we seek to do for God we must seek his guidance through prayer. Jesus did nothing of himself but he sought the Father's will in all things and he was victorious at all times. We must follow his example if we are really to succeed. (John 11:41–42, 17:1)
3. **Stand by your convictions** and refuse to compromise. Many people know in their hearts what God wants them to do, but because of fear of what family, friends or others may say, they quickly stifle what they feel is right and end up in defeat. As I related earlier, when I was asked to sing a folk song, I declined and sang what I knew would glorify God; in so doing a whole new avenue was opened up for me, someone was encouraged, and prayer in our rooms was born.
4. **Don't be afraid to open your door** in the name of Jesus, to those who are genuinely seeking help. As we seek to be guided by God, he helps us to discern real needs in order that we may share his love with those who are without. Hospitality is also a principle by which we extend the Gospel message. (I Tim. 3:2, I Pet. 4:9) As we share him with others we become light to those who are in sin's darkness and they will see and desire him.
5. **Start discussion groups** to stimulate interests and bring to the surface any underlying problems and issues. At first progress may be difficult but sensitivity to different cultural approaches and perseverance will pay off. Individuals can be greatly helped in a group situation even if they do not actively

participate themselves: they hear of situations similar to their own, they see the successful outcome and are encouraged. Bible quizzes and religious films are valuable aids. (Ideas for such groups are suggested in Part II of this book.)

6. **Use social events** which are not necessarily 'religiously' based—by this I mean a coming together to get to know each other and enjoy each others company in a relaxed atmosphere, once again bearing in mind that what may be acceptable for one may not necessarily be understood by another. Having a meal or just a quiet evening together may be a good event to start with, seeking always to forge a closer bond or link. It is God's will that his people should be one with him, and join with each other in a Covenant relationship. Every woman has a part to play in making this possible.

Tretelle E. Carr

Tretelle E. Carr is a retired sister from Netherne hospital in Surrey. She now works in association with the Prison Christian Fellowship and the Women's Prayer Group originally linked to the Mission to London Women's Committee. She is an active member of the West Indian Church Chapel of Truth and is married to Egerton. They have four children.

14. Meeting Asian Women

How would you feel if you heard that an Asian family was coming to live next door? Be honest! We do not have to be racist to wonder about our new neighbours, especially when they come from a different cultural background, and we may be living at quite close quarters. The important thing is to keep an open mind and to expect to form friendships which will expand our horizons and enlarge our understanding.

There are now between half and one million women and girls of South Asian origin living in Britain. Most of them come from India, Pakistan and Bangladesh, with some from Sri Lanka and others of Indian descent from East African countries. Most of these women are British citizens, having a different cultural heritage, but sharing a common national life, now and in the future. Generally speaking they are an underprivileged group, often living in crowded, unattractive urban areas, cut off from the mainstream of society through religious, cultural and linguistic differences.

This is not only a challenge to Christian women in this country: it is also an opportunity. Many of these Asian women have needs that can be met by Christians, but they also have attitudes and skills they can share with us. The centre and focus of Asian life is the family, and it is the women who hold the family together and who teach the next generation to do the same. Though the male dominance in Asian society and the decision-making role of the male head of the family suggest that the women are of no importance, such is not the case. In fact they have a significant but different role—looking after the family life—even when, as in the case of some of my friends, they have long hours and demanding work in the world outside their family. With the concern about the break-up of family life in this country, Asian women may well have a contribution to make in arresting this trend of disintegration as they continue to make their role in the family a priority.

Another area in which Asian women make an outstanding contribution to society as a whole is in their ability to cope with the difficult conditions of our inner cities. Many are, or have been in the past, caught up in the poverty, bad housing, poor health, under-achievement syndrome. In spite of this, they have not necessarily despaired, but have usually managed to keep their families together. Over the years, quite a number of these families have risen above their difficult situation and have begun to prosper. No one should have to live in such disadvantaged conditions; we should do all we can to alleviate inner-city problems. We can, however, admire the qualities that make Asian women work long hours sewing or cleaning so that their families may eat and the bills may be paid. A friend of mine was left a widow with two young daughters and no other near relatives in England. In order to bring up her two children and to keep a comfortable home for them, she has worked 12 to 14 hours a day, mainly for clothing factories.

Family Life

Margaret Wardell, who worked among Asians in Southall for many years, has commented, 'The home and the family are the keystone of Asian culture, and personal friendship also ranks high.' When I asked an Asian friend what she most enjoyed doing she said, 'Visiting friends.' We can take heart when we plan to visit Asian friends; we will receive a warm welcome, and once friendship has been established, they will appreciate coming to our homes, too.

The extended family is the pattern of Asian family life. The different generations live together and as the sons marry they bring their wives into the family home. In Britain some families keep to this traditional way of life, while others— particularly couples who have come here on their own, or those who have been born here—tend to live in nuclear families, with their children. Even so, there are often relatives or friends living temporarily in Asian homes, or paying visits.

Social Customs

In Asian culture there is no social mixing of the sexes. Even husband and wife usually entertain separately and do not express their relationship in public. In Britain friendships *are* being formed between British and Asian couples, but it is best, at least at first, for men to converse with men and women with women. If when visiting we, as women, find a house where only Asian men are living, we should not go in, even if invited. Asians still judge Westerners by what they see in films, so will expect Western women to have freer standards of morality than Asian women. If both men and women are present in the homes we visit, we can accept the invitation to go in, but should sit with the women, or ask to join them if they are in a separate room. Better still, we can find a time when the women are alone in the house; they will then feel at ease to entertain us. If we are visiting as a church team, men and women should visit separately.

The dress of Asian women is both attractive and modest; when we visit, ours should be as well. The different styles of dress are regional as well as religious, so you will probably find Muslims from Bangladesh wearing saris, rather than the tunic and trousers (called *shilwar kamiz*) common in the Punjab of India and in Pakistan.

Most Asians are Muslims, Sikhs, or Hindus, so they have their own restrictions about what they can eat or drink. For Muslims, pigs are unclean, so ham, pork and bacon should not be served. All orthodox Hindus are vegetarians abstaining from eggs and fish as well as meat. No Hindu would ever eat beaf, as cows are sacred animals. Very few Asians drink alcoholic drinks. It is best to discuss what your friend and her family like to eat before preparing the meal. She will appreciate your concern to provide what they will enjoy. Muslims eat only meat which has been slaughtered according to Islamic practice (*halal* meat), so Muslim friends may like to help in the preparation of the meal. Learning how to cook Asian meals widens one's repertoire and may well strengthen the friendship, at the same time producing additional tasty menus! High caste Hindus may not eat or drink with people of another caste, and certainly cannot eat food prepared by Christians. We must be understanding about this, finding other ways than over the kitchen stove and round the dining table to form friendships with them.

When entertaining or being entertained, other surprises may await you. Asian families are units, so even babies and young children come with their parents in response to an invitation, and they expect you to bring your children to their homes. For Asians it is impolite to arrive punctually, so unless the family has become Westernized about time, expect that they will be at least half an hour late. Again, you should do the same when visiting them. Occasionally an Asian family may accept an invitation, but not turn up. For an Asian, it is impolite to refuse even though, for a variety of reasons, he may have no intention of coming. This gives us a sense of anti-climax, even of outrage, and there is a lot of food left over. Try, however, to carry on the friendship as if the incident had not happened; with practice one learns to word invitations in a way which helps detect whether acceptances are genuine!

With the strong family ties, it is not surprising that births, marriages and deaths and the rites of passage which go with them have a great significance. Particularly in the case of funerals, our presence is a sign of both friendship and respect for the person who has died, and for the family. Even if not close friends, we should make very effort to attend. This will not go unnoticed.

Schooling and Medical Care

One problem that arises for Asians in this country is the difficulty in finding places for their children in single-sex schools. Because of the strict segregation of the sexes and the system of arranged marriages, most Asians have a strong preference for single-sex schools, at least for girls of secondary school age. Sometimes we can help with this, not in an official capacity but as friends. A couple of years ago I went with a Bangladeshi friend to an appeal hearing after her daughter had been refused a place in the local single-sex school. The appeal was successful and doing this together helped to cement our friendship. Similarly the closure of most of the hospitals for the treatment of women and children has distressed many Asian women. It may be possible to help them find suitable alternatives, or at least doctors' practices where there are women doctors and where their cultural needs are understood.

It is very important that concerned Christians in local churches should co-operate with the different branches of the social services in the area. I am reminded of an occasion some years ago when the inner-city church of which I am a member was co-operating in a housing survey organized by the local neighbourhood centre. I was asked to look at some flats in an old property. I found only one flat habitable in which were living a Pakistani couple with a baby of a few months old. It was damp and dangerous (part of the ceiling had fallen down over the bed, narrowly missing the baby). The mother was alone all day, as her husband was working. They had recently come to Britain and had no other relatives here. The other Asians in the neighbourhood were from Bangladesh, a different language area. I was able to report on the housing conditions, but, more importantly as I had lived in Pakistan I was able to get to know the family and to continue visiting the mother until they were re-housed in another area.

Differing Needs

It is unwise to try to put people into categories, for we are all individuals and have vastly differing needs. However, because Asian families are still in a transitional stage of settlement in Britain, it may be helpful when considering their needs to think of the different age-groups of Asian women in this country.

There is a large number of older women, some of whom have been widowed since coming here. Many have not learned to speak English and do not go out of their homes except on special occasions, when they are accompanied by their families. Many of them did not have the benefit of schooling, so they are not literate even in their own language. Margaret Wardell remarks, 'Those who are illiterate are not necessarily unintelligent. Most girls brought up in Asia a generation ago never had the opportunity to attend a school, but they often have considerable poise and patience and are shrewd and thrifty.' When friendships are formed, there are a number of ways in which we can help such women. They may have learned some English from their children, but most of them would like to be able to speak and understand more. English classes are usually available in areas where Asians are living and we can encourage our Asian friends to attend, perhaps taking them along and introducing them on their first visit. For older women, the classes may not be the best way of learning, and perhaps teaching in their homes is more suitable; it is also a good way of forming friendships.

We may like to consider learning an Asian language ourselves. This should not be combined with an Asian learning English but should be a separate project, with a helper who already speaks some English. The LAMP (Language Acquisition Made Practical) method developed by Tom and

Elizabeth Brewster is very helpful, particularly because it emphasises culture as well as language.[1] I spent a brief time learning Bengali using the LAMP method, and my helper has become a personal friend. When we finished our last lesson together, she began to ask me how Muslim and Christian beliefs differed; I have had many opportunities of sharing with her since then, including Bible studies in her home and visits to the church.

Older women with families may need advice concerning their teenage children. There was no developed teenage culture when they grew up in Asian homes, and they may appreciate help in understanding it. They may also be worried about opportunities for further education and job openings. A Bengali-speaking friend and I recently visited a widowed mother who was worried about whether her son should stay on at college and what sort of job his studies would lead to. We were able to get advice from the college and to put the family in touch with the careers officer. There are often forms to fill in and official letters to write, and we can assist with these.

Sometimes our help may be of an even more practical nature. I remember visiting a friend and finding her kitchen drain blocked and the floor awash with water, which was steadily rising! I was able to talk to the emergency plumber and get across a sense of urgency which she, with limited English, was finding difficult. It is not always possible to be around when we are needed, but building up friendships, mutual confidence and regular visiting will help.

A number of Asian families are bringing girls over as brides for their sons. It is thought that these girls are more ready to comply with Asian cultural standards than those influenced by Western life styles. Usually they live with their husbands in the extended family, at least at first, where their relationship with their mother-in-law is very important. She organises both the household duties and the outside contacts.

Girls coming to Britain and living alone with their husbands may suffer from extreme homesickness. One friend described the first few months here like this: 'I was alone at home all day. I watched the television and I cried when I thought of my parents. With them we were such a big family; we were all together. Now I am so lonely.' We need to be imaginative in knowing how to help. Another friend looks back to the day when an English friend took her to Kew Gardens as the turning-point in her adaptation to living in Britain.

Young girls born in Britain may have special problems if they are brought up in traditional extended families. Margaret Wardell thinks that 'rebellion of Asian young people against what they regard as the restrictive attitude of their parents is increasing.' As they meet their British school-fellows and form friendships with them, there is an inevitable clash of cultures; many Asian children are searching for their identity. It is not surprising if they rebel against their lack of freedom to choose, particularly in finding a marriage partner. Arranged marriages are still common practice, but perhaps this is not as coercive as it seems, since the interests of the girl are carefully considered and decisions are made jointly. Some families have found a satisfactory compromise when a couple are attracted to each other by 'arranging' a marriage between them within the traditional framework. Sometimes, however, a girl has to choose between obeying her family and marrying the man of her choice. Marriage without consent leads to much unhappiness, and both the family and the girl concerned need help and support from their friends. Another cause of family clashes is when a girl wants to go out to work and to pursue a profession, while the family wants her to stay at home until she is married.

Asian Religions

Most Asian women are glad to talk about their religion and will be interested to hear about ours too. Once friendships have been formed and confidence established, there will be opportunity to share our beliefs. It will be best to let our friends tell us what they believe, then we can tell them about

our faith in Jesus Christ. It is helpful if we know a little about
their religions; then we can share what our faith means to
us, without compromising the truth, but emphasising what
will be most helpful.

Muslims

The majority of Asians in this country are Muslims. Islam is
strongly monotheistic, proclaiming that giving God a
'partner' is the greatest sin. It is understandable that our
discussions together should focus on the person and work
of Jesus, whom they consider to have been a prophet, but
not divine. The Qur'an is the holy book of Islam, believed to
have been the exact Words of Allah (Arabic word for God)
sent down to their prophet Muhammad. For Muslims it is
God's final revelation, the foundation of all their beliefs and
practices. They believe the Bible to be God's previous
messages to his people, but to have been altered and cor-
rupted by Jews and Christians.

   Muslims have strong, well-defined arguments refuting the
Christian faith. We will be wise not to enter into fruitless,
heated discussions, only correcting gross misconceptions
about what Christians do believe. We must keep in mind that
when Muslims are converted it is usually through one or
more of these factors: Christians showing friendship and
kindness; reading the Bible; and God speaking directly
through visions, dreams, or miraculous healing. We should
encourage our friends to read Scripture (the gospel of
Matthew is a good place to start) and we should pray that
God will reveal himself to our Muslim friends in a powerful
and personal way.

Hindus

Hinduism is an ancient religion of many gods, whose stories
are recounted in a number of holy books. Hindu women
have their own special deity, usually in Britain Ram or
Krishna; they may have a room in their homes set aside for
worship and prayer and will certainly have a shrine depict-

ing the god. Stories of gods such as Ram and Sita are enacted at Hindu festivals, so our Hindu friends will be familiar with them, although they may not know much about the philosophical aspects of their faith.

Hindus believe that they are locked into a cycle of existences, each one determined by behaviour in the previous one. This is the doctrine of *karma* and reincarnation. You may be surprised how readily your Hindu friend accepts and believes in Jesus Christ, but, as Margaret Wardell says, 'Hinduism is all-embracing. It is possible to believe anything and to be a Hindu—so Jesus can be absorbed into the Hindu system as long as he can be put alongside the other gods and doctrines.' It is a much bigger and more difficult step for a Hindu to accept Jesus as the only way, but we must firmly insist on his uniqueness when talking with our Hindu friends.

Sikhs

There are also a considerable number of Sikhs living in Britain. Their religion arose from Hinduism through the teaching of Guru Nanak, and they greatly reverence their holy book, the *Granth Sahib*. They are noted for good living and service to the community. Many of the early Sikhs, including three of their ten gurus, gave their lives for their faith, which may help Sikhs understand something of Christ's sacrificial death. They also believe that a divine Spirit enlightened the writers of the *Granth* and works to some measure in the lives of Sikh followers, so there may be helpful discussion on the presence and work of the Holy Spirit.

RWF Wootton, writing on Asian religions in *Jesus Christ the Only Way,* summarised:

> We may find much to admire in the Hindu's reverence for life and search for peace, in the Buddhist's longing for enlightenment and moral excellence and in the Sikh's practical goodness to those in need, and be challenged in our own faith and practice thereby . . . the one thing that is unique to Christianity is Christ himself.[2]

We should encourage Sikhs and Hindus to read the Bible, starting perhaps with the gospels of Luke and John. As most Asian families are accustomed to looking at videos of Hindi films, it may also be helpful to show them some of the Christian videos which are now available.

Challenges to the Church

If meeting Asian women is to lead not only to friendship and to sharing our beliefs together, but also to conversions, our churches must be ready and welcoming. For Asian women (whether Muslims, Hindus, or Sikhs) to come to a Christian church is a very big step; this is especially so for Hindus, who are not accustomed to any kind of congregational worship. We must be ready to explain and interpret our forms of worship and the meaning their convey to believers, as well as making sure that our friends are welcomed with warmth and friendship. Perhaps we should also consider just how well the worship and fellowship in our churches reflect the universal message of the Christian faith.

Sadly, Britain is not now a country where the Gospel can easily be heard. We must recognise that Christians are a small minority of British people. An Asian Christian friend commented recently on our empty churches. It is understandable if Asian women of other faiths wonder why we visit them, who practise their own religions sincerely, but ignore our fellow countrywomen, who seem to have no faith at all. If we are wanting to share the Gospel with Asian women, perhaps we need to be seen to be reaching out to the whole population of the area and to be expressing our concern about falling standards and permissiveness around us. Can we personally, and British Christians as a whole, respond to these challenges?

Anne Cooper

Notes

[1] E. Thomas and Elizabeth Brewster, *Language Acquisition Made Practical* (Lingua House, 1976).
[2] Patrick Sookhdeo, ed., *Jesus Christ the Only Way* (Paternoster Press, 1978), p.75.

Anne Cooper is the compiler of the study course called Ishmael My Brother, an informative guide for Christian workers overseas and at home who are particularly concerned to reach Moslems. The understanding and perception about cross-cultural friendship and ministry that shine out of this chapter are based on many years of nursing and mission experience in Pakistan with BMMF Interserve. Anne Cooper now lives in London.

15. Women in the Arts

For many members of the Christian artistic community in London it seemed that Alan and I just popped out of nowhere. Suddenly, or so it seemed, we were running a weekly supper party at the Arts Centre Group and seeing people in our home for prayer. But, of course, the Lord never does anything without groundwork.

While studying in California I met an actor at church. Because of our common roots in Britain we established a friendship which soon led to marriage. Having been involved in outreach before, I felt a new anticipation for serving the Lord rise in my heart. I realised that as Alan pursued his career in Hollywood we would be drawn into circles where few people would even consider Christianity seriously. Yet it seemed we were diverted from that course when Alan left acting and gave himself to Christian service. Soon we were on our way back to England.

We began to discover other actors in our church in London and quite naturally began to support them in prayer, counsel and friendship. Our new friends came often to our home, talking about conflicts in their careers and personal lives. They in return shared our burdens and concerns. Alan and I usually work together chatting and interceding with different people. We find great joy in working as a team. (I am very privileged to have a husband who respects my experience and training and who is not intimidated by it.)

As friendships developed, the old anticipation for reaching people in the arts began to stir in us again. We knew God was moving us in that direction. But we knew we had to wait, because artists—especially—are wary of having their privacy and friendship abused. Alan and I and a couple of actor friends began to pray.

The first breakthrough came when a friend got a good part in a show in London's West End and asked Alan to lead a Bible study in his dressing-room at the theatre. During these weeks, the group saw how God could move through their prayers to lift oppression in the atmosphere and to touch the people working with them.

Open House

Then we were invited to attend the regular actors' meetings at the Arts Centre Group (ACG). ACG is a centre for encouraging and supporting Christians involved in the Arts. At one meeting the discussion led to the idea of having the premises open late, after shows ended, so that artists could unwind with friends there instead of at a London night spot. Everyone was excited about the idea. We all started looking around the room for volunteers. This work meant someone's being there from early evening to the early hours of the next morning. Those who were working days felt it was beyond them. Suddenly, my husband spoke up from across the room, 'We'll do it!' It was one of the few times we didn't consult together first, and initially my heart sank. Food was to be prepared, which meant planning menus, shopping and organising meals for about 40 people each week. Then there was our one-year-old son to consider. But deep in my heart I knew this was what the Lord wanted, and after a pause I confirmed Alan's offer. However, I did manage to delay the opening for a couple of months to enable me to find cooks, helpers, and a regular babysitter.

We called the project 'Open House'. It seemed as if the evenings just happened. But the preparation started around four in the afternoon, when Alan Melville would go straight from work to the supermarket and buy the provisions for the evening's menu. Usually, I would meet him there and we would drive together to the ACG. Often, transport was a problem, so at times he would have to make his own way. I would arrive harassed and bedraggled to find the initial preparations well in hand.

From 6 o'clock to 9 pm, we would busy ourselves making a couple of different entrees; two or three desserts; a home-made soup; and something that could be eaten as a hearty snack. The quality of the food was important, every bit as much as the spiritual atmosphere. I believe that artistic beauty and balance should be visible qualities in the life of a Christian. Good food graciously and lovingly provided is an effective way of showing people you care about them. We wouldn't think of giving Jesus over-brewed coffee and old biscuits. Alan (who is an experienced cook) and I had great fun searching for unique and tasty recipes.

We did charge for the cost of the food. ACG gave us a grant of £25 to start with. I did not feel the need to be reimbursed for our labour, so we figured the cost for each portion and added a quarter or third more for margin. No matter what the crowd was like, small or large, we always had enough return to supply a complete menu for the next week. Never did we have to go back and ask for more, or give out of our own pockets. Since I am not a business person, I saw that as an indication of the Lord's blessing.

At 9.30 pm the candles would be lit, and a delicious aroma would waft from the kitchen into the cosy dining room. The scene was set. Alan and I always aimed to steer the conversation towards our faith but ACG members were not made to feel that their friends would be pounced upon by wild-eyed evangelists! It was a time for allowing the Lord to do his work. That meant there was always something positive going on.

Each evening was unique. Sometimes the air was filled with happy, light-hearted conversations. At other times, we would be engaged in deep discussion about God and human need. Each evening Alan and I and the other helpers made a point of greeting people at each table. Our aim was to be sensitive to the moving of the Holy Spirit. We looked for places in people's lives where we could sense God was at work and focussed our energies there. This saves a lot of wasted energy. It also helps to maintain a gracious yet powerful atmosphere.

To obtain the sense that the Holy Spirit is present, moving, and ruling in a situation requires the essential groundwork of intercessory prayer before and during the event. This is where the real hard labour is done. There was a noticeable difference and lack of peace on the evenings when we had not managed to gather for prayer beforehand. We quickly learned how important prayer was for the work at Open House, regardless of how hard it was to finish preparations in time.

As we moved from table to table, often entering into probing conversation with people more highly educated than ourselves, confidence in the unquenchable light of God's love and truth became vital. Conversation with an artist can be challenging and exhilarating. The artistic mind is trained to analyse. Artists study life in detail, probing into things which the average person passes by. A true artist— whether painter, poet, or actor—can look into something common, examine it and enable you to see something rare and inspiring. Good art will make you return to it, to look and think again, until you discover something new.

Artists can be uncomfortable. They will not tolerate trite explanations and are offended by platitudes. Like explorers, artists will dare to experiment with colour, sound, move-ment and emotions. An artist will dare to walk the tight-rope between disaster and grace, just to create. How important it is when dealing with this kind of temperament to have a rooted confidence that there is no challenge too great, no honest doubt unanswerable by God. The Lord loves us too much to let our puny objections repel him. One must be armed with the knowledge that God has promised to be found by those who seek. There is always a way to bring people to an understanding of who the Lord is. Then when they see him, the choice is theirs whether they accept him or reject him. Our task is to learn the language they speak in order to help them understand.

How important it is not to compromise the purity and strength of God's truth. A person who works with artists must be open to discuss everything and yet always stay true to their understanding of God's Word. Conversations led to friendships, conversions and discipling based at our home. How well new Christians adjusted and remained in the church depended very much on how closely the person who brought them to the Open House stayed in relationship with them. Though churches were glad to receive new people, few in the congregation were able to relate to artists. Having to work odd hours often keeps artists on the fringes of church life: their work is often at nights and week-ends. Only a few churches have realised that there are segments of society that cannot meet the standard church schedule. Sometimes even clergy cannot relate to the artist's lifestyle.

An artists' clique seems to serve as a necessary support. Unfortunately, these may be groups left to shepherd themselves. Cliques without a mature leadership related to the mainstream of the church often become introverted, leading people to disillusionment and loss of faith. Sometimes artists resist the interference of a caring pastor because they assume that his godly wisdom is irrelevant to an artist's needs.

In our situation, the clergy were glad to see some direction evolve in reaching artists. They trusted our group to get on with it. While we appreciated such trust, Alan and I always had to take the initiative to communicate with the main body and leadership of the church. Though generally caring and loving, they were often unaware of the demands being made upon us. For instance, though our church had an organised baby-sitting team for church functions, our needs had to be met from within our group. Needless to say, the guy who offered was bribed with a hearty meal! The discovery of new and loving friendships such as his became the keynote at Open House. In this environment people felt free to share their concerns.

Women had their own special needs. One woman among many was hung up about Christianity and sexual morality. She couldn't understand the logic of it. Then she feared not being able to live up to Christian standards. Setting aside the scriptural demands, Alan talked about the insecurity and pain so often caused by relating sexually to someone without the protection of a lasting marriage commitment. The real release came when Alan assured her that God could help her maintain sexual purity even though she had already become sexually active, because God had done the same for him. Not only had the Lord given Alan self-control, he had restored in him a freshness and purity that Alan had lost. A few days later, while attending church with a friend from Open House, she had the courage to come to Christ and put her trust in his sustaining power. Immediately, she started to share her faith with her theatrical friends and became a faithful helper at Open House.

Another woman was a young Christian when we first met her. She had a wonderful love and faith in the Lord, but she felt rootless. She didn't feel she fitted in anywhere. This was not only inhibiting, but drastically affected her acting career. Her inward instability led to spiralling bouts of confusion. She needed to gain perspective and comfort. Although she linked up with a home group at church, she was unable to identify with the women who befriended her.

The real challenge for us came when she started to confide her fears. It was a tough time, but then one day the light dawned. With the counsel of some other Christian friends she became convinced that a pure, uncomplicated Christian lifestyle was the only way to health and security. A new stability manifested itself in her life increasingly from them on.

For others, the challenges related more to their careers. Not only do artists and performers have to learn how to listen to the Holy Spirit when they make career choices, but they have to deal also with the negative views of the Church, which has taught for many years that Christians should not be involved in the arts. My mother turned down an arts scholarship because her pastor felt she might have to paint nudes! Others think it better to join a Christian evangelistic team than to 'play the fiddle while Rome burns'.

One young woman asked us to pray about whether she should join such a team. To her surprise we discouraged her. Other friends thought she would be strengthened by such a godly environment! They overlooked the spiritual battles she was walking into and the intense personal demands ministry requires. From growing up in a minister's household, I have come to the conclusion that people need a deep call to ministry for which God will anoint them. Our friend spent many miserable months wrestling with a role she wasn't equipped for. As Christians we must avoid categorising people. Rather we must be willing to wait on the leading of the Spirit to reveal what each of us should do. Ironically, as the young woman recovered the time lost in her career, she proved to be an effective evangelist within her vocation.

Too often in our zeal to disciple people, we have imposed sweeping standards and are insensitive to the hardship it brings. For example, we would never counsel a doctor who has spent years of gruelling training and sacrifice to leave his profession and find something else. Yet, counsellors have turned to artists who have spent tedious years of training and career building and told them they need to find work in a more wholesome field. What do they do? They need a call from the Lord, spoken to their own heart and blessed with a gift of faith, before making such a step.

Paul, who is seen often as the stern and uncompromising zealot of the Early Church, manifested great compassion and foresight. In I Corinthians 7:17–24 he apparently faced the situation where people were feeling constrained to change their lifestyle radically. Marriages were being threatened; slaves were wanting to leave their ungodly and often debauched masters. Foreseeing the pain such sudden changes would cause new Christians he said, 'Each one should remain in the situation which he was in when God called him. Were you a slave when you were called? Don't let it trouble you—although if you can gain your freedom, do so.' (I Cor. 7:20, 21) Paul was not endorsing slavery. He was encouraging gentleness and long-suffering towards people. Look how rapidly Christianity spread throughout the world because of the far-reaching effects of people who stayed in their allotted role in life! Do we endorse much of what the arts and media promote? No, but we do have a responsibility to redeem what has become corrupt.

This requires more Christians being willing to take the challenge of supporting those in the arts, teaching them to push back the darkness in their own lives and in their profession.

Areas of Difficulty

A major battle for women in the arts is the constant assault against dignity of being female. I believe this is an all-out offensive to humiliate and degrade women—to divest us of any personal dignity and purity. The Devil has often succeeded in using the arts to deface the image of God and the reflection of divine purity and beauty embodied especially in woman. Directors, photographers and choreographers who have no sense of responsibility often allow women to be sworn at, man-handled, and undressed just to produce an 'artistic' result. Rather than lose their jobs, women have submitted to this. Their training has often insisted on breaking down inhibitions which might block 'creative power'. When these women become Christians, they need support, to challenge all this and act according to their Christian conscience in an often hostile environment.

Another area of attack against women in the arts is coming from the radical feminist stereotype, which produces an image of a 'liberated' woman who is able and willing to withstand all the abuse a man can offer, to curse with the best, and to be sexually indiscriminate. Many women have succumbed to that view and are ashamed to register objection at the treatment they receive. I have even heard a young Christian woman use foul language for the sake of effect from the speakers' podium. There is no freedom where, because of current trends, women are ashamed to protect their dignity and stand up for personal values.

As Christian women we have a real and valid basis for our confidence, something tangible and unique to offer our sisters in the world. We belong to God. We have been redeemed, purified, and sanctified by the blood of Christ. No higher price could have been paid for us. Secular feminism will always fall short because its basis is equality with men, rather than relationship with God. As Christians, our dignity is not based on assertiveness, one person competing against another, but upon a divine and eternal gift of grace, which can never be upset by the passing influences of this life because it is based in eternity. We rest in the knowledge that we were specially created by the love of God. We are creatures in our own right, with our own gifts and graces to serve others.

Breaking New Ground

There seems to be a recurring theme in the way God has worked in my life. He periodically calls me to break new ground for a new work, raise up leadership and then move on. This challenges my natural desire to mother and to hold on to those whom God has brought into my life. It disciplines the inclination to become comfortable in an established work and self-secure in the acceptance of those around me. We naturally recoil from leaving loved ones behind to do something new once again somewhere else.

But we are called to give without grasping.

The challenge to move on from our involvements in London finally came. The Lord recommissioned Alan to focus on a performing career, both secular and Christian, which will draw us even more closely to artists who need ministry. Currently we are in Los Angeles seeking the Lord day by day as he opens up his will for us.

The work at the Open House in London continues. It has matured from our haphazard beginnings to a more organised system, with a team of people sharing the responsibility of ministry to artists. Others have caught the vision and a similar project of outreach among London's theatre-goers has been established in London's West End. ACG also has local groups in different parts of the UK.

La Donna Elliot

La Donna Elliot and her husband initiated Open House at the Christian Arts Centre Group in London. Her vision was to create a friendly atmosphere where Christians in the professional arts could bring their friends for a meal and to talk, especially after late-night shows. With a small team of volunteers, they were available on a weekly basis to share their faith and counsel anyone in need. While Open House continues, La Donna and Alan have returned to the USA and are now based in California.

16. Women in Sport

I was brought up in a Christian family. At church one Sunday the preacher asked anyone who wanted to accept Jesus Christ as friend and Saviour to raise their hands. I nudged my father, who was sitting next to me, and asked him if it would be OK if I raised mine—he of course said yes. I was seven years old. Nothing miraculously changed. No thunderbolts, no flashing lights, but within me a seed had been sown. Unfortunately my seed didn't get much water between the ages of 7 and 17. I knew I was saved; I went to church every Sunday, but that was about the extent of it. God was not number one in my life.

This came to my attention on my first trip to America in December 1981. Before I left, my father asked me if I was taking a Bible. After I had made some feeble excuses about not having a travel Bible, he went out and bought me one. He then told me to read it every day. I found this no problem the first three weeks I was in America, as I had a room to myself and would read a chapter before I got out of bed. However, for the next few weeks, I was playing in a few amateur golf tournaments and had to share rooms with several different girls. That was a different story. I didn't exactly try to hide my light under a bushel, but under the bedclothes, or in the bathroom! What God was showing me here was just how feeble my faith had become. I wasn't frightened to admit that I was a Christian, but I wasn't putting God in his rightful place. I wasn't at all discerning about what I watched on TV, or what music I listened to. God, however, doesn't try to change everything at once, but slowly, little by little.

The first major change came about six months later. My father died, and for the first time in my life, instead of relying on him, I had to rely on God. That was when God really began to work in my life.

I had first started playing golf when I was 17. I was on holiday in Scotland at the time, and a friend of my father's was giving my father a lesson, when he switched his attention to me and showed me how to hit a few shots. I must have hit them quite well because it prompted him to say 'Oh, it's a shame Kitrina didn't take the game up earlier; I think she could be quite good!' How on earth he could tell after seeing a beginner hit a few shots I shall never know, but later that evening my father asked me if I would like to leave school and play golf for a year and see how well I could do? Rather a strange thing for a father to ask, you may say! On the face of it, I would agree, but my father had been a semi-pro footballer and knew a lot about sport. He also realised that unlike many other pro-sports, when you are finished at 25 to 30, with golf you can play top class until you are nearly 50. He also knew that I shared his love for all sports and a lot of his natural ability, and so it wasn't such a gamble as it might at first have seemed. However, he put no pressure on me by saying that I must become a pro or that I must succeed, only that I could play and practise, and that at the end of a year if I didn't like it, or didn't like playing full time, I could go back to studying, still having a game that I would be able to play for the rest of my life. At the end of the summer holidays, I went to school and announced that I was leaving at Christmas to become a golfer. 'Oh,' I can remember the teachers saying, 'and are you very good at golf?' 'No,' I replied, 'I've never played before!'

I left school in 1977, and after Christmas joined a small club in Bristol where I started playing and practising every day. Because I was playing so much, and having coaching every week from a top professional, my game improved rapidly, in fact rather miraculously. (During the first year my handicap went down from 36 to 19.) One year off became two. The next year my handicap was down to three and I was good enough to win our county championship. The next year I was playing to one, and won the Scottish Girls' Open Stroke Play. At the Balmore Bakeries Trophy I was runner up in the English under-23s and was picked to play for the full England side. I was to line up alongside women who had been playing for 10, 15 or 20 years. The next year, after a winter of playing in America, I won the British Amateur Championship, beating golfers from all over the world—the most prestigious tournament that a woman can win in golf. By winning this I was also picked to play for Great Britain in the biennial match against the United States of America in Denver, Colorado. My biggest ambition had come to fruition. The only sad part was that my father had died two months earlier. During the next year, however, I found it very hard to motivate myself, due partly to my father's death and also to the fact that as an amateur, I didn't have any more mountains to climb; I had reached my goal. Also, since my father's death, it was more difficult for me financially. While he had been alive, he had supported my golf. Now I was having to do hundreds of jobs to pay my expenses, which of course meant that I wasn't devoting as much time as I ought to the golf.

I came to the decision in 1984 that either I should stop playing golf and get a full-time job, or stop doing all these jobs I had been doing, and turn professional.

I realised that God hadn't given me all this talent to give up golf at this stage, and so I turned professional. However, I had no sponsors to help pay my expenses, no endorsements as extra revenue, and on top of that I had a rather large bank overdraft, due to a winter's practice in Portugal.

The first tournament I played in as a professional golfer was the Ford Ladies' Classic at Woburn. It was the curtain-raiser to the 1984 ladies' golf season. The ladies' golf circuit travels from country to country each week, from the beginning of May until the end of October, visiting countries such as Sweden, Holland, Belgium, Germany, France, Portugal, and Spain—as well as many venues in England, Scotland, Ireland, Jersey, and Guernsey.

During the 1984 season, we played for nearly half a million pounds in prize money. This has risen since then, to just under a million pounds, due to the success of the circuit. At the Ford classic in 1984, the total purse for the event was £20,000, the first prize £3,000. I didn't really think I stood a chance of winning, this being my first event as a pro. I was just happy to compete and to win some money. By the end of the week, everything had changed; I had won first prize! I could now play the whole year if necessary, without a sponsor. I could also pay off my overdraft, and things began to look brighter.

During that first year on tour, I played exceptionally well and began to see how God could use a Christian in the world of professional sport. Kids think that by wearing the same football shirt as Gary Lineker they will be able to play football well, or by using the same tennis racket Boris Becker uses they will be able to play tennis superbly, or by wearing the same running shoes Seb Coe uses they will be able to run as fast. Adults can be just as gullible. Millions wouldn't be spent every year on advertising if it didn't influence people. We are being told all the time what the top sports people are eating, drinking, driving, wearing—even what credit cards they are using! In turn, as professionals, we are being watched by people wanting to copy our every move in the hope that some of the success or glamour will rub off. What a great opportunity this is for Christians to witness and to point the way to Jesus. However, along with the opportunity comes a great responsibility, despite all our imperfections and mistakes, for others will judge us and our Saviour by the way we live our lives. It is a challenge and of course we can only succeed if we walk in the power and strength of Jesus Christ. The first opportunity I had for sharing my faith was after I won the first tournament. One of the other golfers also wrote in one of the golf magazines. During the post-match interviews she asked me how I had coped with the pressure. In all honesty I told her that I had prayed. 'No!' she said. 'Seriously?' Well, I didn't get much mileage there, but looking back I can see that I had to wait for God's time. I was ready, if the journalists were willing to listen. However, I was aware that I would have to be very careful what I said, as there are a lot of writers who would make fun of our faith in print and do a lot more harm than good.

During that first year I was interviewed nearly every week by one paper or another, plus several radio stations and local TV. My elder sister Karen, aware of the opportunities, said to me, 'You know, you really should be mentioning that you are a Christian.' I agreed. So when I next had an interview, we prayed that if it was God's will that I should speak out, the interviewer would ask me something so that I could bring faith into the conversation. John, a reporter from Radio Bristol, turned up about twenty minutes later. I was sure God was going to move, but the conversation went something like this.

JOHN: Well, Kitrina, a very successful year so far, where have you been recently?

ME: I've just returned from a week in Sweden and a week in Birmingham.

JOHN: And how did you do?

ME: I won the tournament in Sweden, and was top pro at the Belfry.

JOHN: What were your scores?

ME: I shot 71, 71, 74, 70 in Sweden and 80, 75, 74, 69 in the other.

JOHN: The 69 sounds good?

ME: Yeah, it was a course record, it's probably the best round of golf I've ever played.

JOHN: And how much did you win?

ME: About £3,800 for the Swedish open, about £3,500 for the European open.

JOHN: Well, thank you, very much. Goodbye.

John left, and with that my sister came running in, 'Well—what did you say?' I explained to Karen that he hadn't asked me anything that could prompt a flood of Christian answers.

I continued to pray before each encounter with the press and felt that when God knew the time was right he would move. A couple of months later, a friendly reporter from the *Daily Mail* asked if he could have an interview. I said yes, and we sat and chatted for about an hour, mainly about golf.

He then asked 'And what do you do in your spare time?'

I replied, 'Oh, I paint, play the guitar, listen to music, read.'

When I got to 'read' he interrupted, 'What are you reading at the moment?'

Here was the moment I'd been waiting for.

'A book called *The Holy Spirit and You*,' I said.

Looking rather puzzled, he asked 'What's the Holy Spirit?'

For the next forty minutes we discussed my faith, how I became a Christian, and what God meant to me. The result of this interview was a full-page article in the *Daily Mail*, beautifully written, saying I was a Christian, and explaining how I read my Bible. This same article was then used by the Women's Professional Golf Association in their yearbook as my personal profile. These books are handed out at all the tournaments we play. I had left the situation in God's hands, and he had not only made sure I was given a clear representation, but that maximum use was made from it.

One of the biggest problems facing me during my first year on tour was that I wasn't getting much teaching or fellowship. Due to the nature of golf, we are often travelling or playing on Sundays. For some Christians, having to work on the sabbath would be unacceptable. But each of us faces the question of what we will and will not do on Sundays. My ideal Sunday would be spent worshipping and studying. However, I think every one of us should look to God and not to others about these things. For this reason I do play on

Sundays. For me, the day itself is irrelevent. It is the time that is important. I prayed about the fact that I felt like a spiritual gypsy, about how I felt I was missing the guidance, fellowship and support which are part of the structure of a normal Christian life. My needs were first met through my sister, who kept me supplied with books, tapes and the odd earful when she thought I needed a rebuke. I also kept bumping into mature Christians on my travels. On buses, trains, airplanes, in fact in the most odd places I would often find someone to talk to.

Then a friend of my mother's who worked in a Christian bookshop sent me sports-related Christian books. One particular book I found interesting was *A Whole New Ball Game* by Gerald Williams, the BBC tennis commentator. In the book he mentioned an organisation called Christians in Sport. This was formed as a result of a group of sportsmen visiting a seminar of Christian sportsmen in the USA, and seeing the need for a similar organisation in Britain. Some weeks later Stuart Weir, the secretary of CIS, wrote asking if there were any ways that they could be of service to me. There were plenty! The main way they were able to help immediately was by offering me accommodation with Christian families. (I can't tell you how much nicer it is to stay in a Christian home than in hotel rooms every week.) But as well as the benefits for me, God had other plans.

One example was in Europe. CIS made a contact with a Christian woman who lived near the course where we were to play. Although Marianne was a Christian, her husband was not and would not even agree to go to church with her. So Marianne had been praying that as her husband wouldn't go to church, God would send Christians into her home. At that point CIS rang her to ask if she would put up a Christian golfer who was playing in a big tournament later in the year. Marianne agreed, thinking it would be great to have a Christian come to stay. Not knowing any of her prayers, I rang her to see if it would be possible for my boyfriend to stay too, since he was hoping to caddy for me. Marianne said she would be delighted, and to herself said 'Now *two* Christians coming to stay!' Marianne then went back and told her husband that Kitrina Douglas was coming to stay.

'How on earth do you know her?' he asked.

'Oh, she's a Christian,' she replied.

When I arrived, not only was the house close to the course—actually on the fifth hole, but Jan, Marianne's husband, was the course manager! During the week we spent time talking to them all. I didn't think I'd been witnessing in any sort of obvious way, but when we came to leave, Marianne gave me a small gift. Inside the card she wrote, 'Thank you for being such a good witness in my home.' She then told me of her prayer, which really encouraged me.

During the last two years, we have been able to start a fellowship group on tour. There were three of us to begin with: Jane Connachan, who has been a Christian for several years; Alison Nicolas, who became a Christian in 1985, and myself. Since those small beginnings, several girls have wanted to come along to our meetings, and many others have made decisions to follow Christ.

The first girl I was able to bring to the Lord was called Sue. During the Men's British Open, I was working on one of the exhibition stands in the tented village. After work one evening Sue came up to me looking worried, asking if I had seen Bridget, a girl who was to give her accommodation that night. I was very tired after being on the stand all day; and it was getting late. I wasn't really wanting to 'do the Christian thing' and invite her to stay with us, but I said that if she was stuck she could come round. I honestly thought she would find somewhere else to stay, but as we drove into the drive of the small cottage some of us had rented for the week, who should pull up beside us but Sue!

I took her in and gave her something to eat, and then we all went to bed. The girl I was sharing a room with had a bad back and was sleeping on the floor in the lounge, so Sue was able to have the bed next to mine.

At lights out, we started talking. The discussion moved to

the flight we had had from Germany the previous week when the plane had suddenly dropped several thousand feet; for about half an hour everything had been quite frightening.

'Well, I don't know about you,' I said, 'but I wasn't really worried; I knew where I was going'.

This was the beginning of a discussion on Christianity which lasted well into the small hours. The outcome was well worth waiting for. At about 2.30 am Sue accepted Jesus Christ as her Saviour.

There have been other stories like this, and now we have about twelve women who have actually made commitments to Jesus.

I can now see that God has placed me in golf for many purposes. It wasn't by luck or by chance. Jesus said, 'Go into all the world and preach the good news to all creation' (Mark 16:15). This doesn't mean just in Third-World countries. What about our towns, villages, neighbours? I believe God puts Christians in all walks of life—in offices, factories, as doctors, dentists, road sweepers, pilots, in sports, music and the arts . . . If we all go overseas, who will tell people around us the Good News—the people in the queue at the supermarket or living next door?

A reporter for the *Guardian* once said to me after I'd been talking to her about Jesus, 'Kitrina, if you feel this way, why don't you become a missionary?' I replied 'I am one'.

Kitrina Douglas

Kitrina Douglas is a professional golfer who lives in Bristol. She took up golf at the late age of 17 when her father took her along to one of his golf lessons. Kitrina, who was hoping to become a professional actress, was soon hooked on the game and left school to play full time. She has an impressive amateur record—British Champion in 1982, Portuguese Champion in 1983—and won the 1986 Mitsubishi Colt Cars Jersey Open.

17. Reaching Older Women

How old is old? A lot depends on the age of the other person. Perhaps 30 seems old to one, 60 to another, and 80 to others. One is still young at 70; another is old at 60. But most church meetings for older people cover an age range from 60 to 90 years, with a few in their fifties. The increasing population in this bracket ought to represent one of the growing edges of the Church's ministry.

In the last 30 years there has been an explosion in studies on ageing and the elderly, but attitudes in society are slow to change. Those between 60 and 90 are lumped together as a group as if their needs and interests were identical, but it only takes a little imagination to appreciate the vast differences between people born 30 years apart.

Most men and women between 60 and 70 are still active, perhaps working, still involved in the community and able to face and adapt to the major changes involved in retirement, lower income, and some physical limitations. They still have the capacity to build on past knowledge and skills and tackle new things. The sixties decade can be a new beginning, holding the possibility of more leisure and new doors to enter. Those in this age group should be encouraged to face the challenges of a new phase of life and perhaps find that the Lord has a new role for them in the church community. It must not be assumed that from now on they will identify happily with those in their eighties and nineties.

Many enter their seventies with the same vigour they had in their sixties, but gradually changes begin. Three-quarters of those over 70 are affected by some degree of chronic illness that restricts them; arthritis, heart disease, hypertension and diabetes are the most common. Movement becomes restricted, sight and hearing may deteriorate, poor circulation makes it harder to keep warm, and there is a lower tolerance to pain.

Mentally, people begin to think and react more slowly. It usually takes longer to absorb new ideas and skills, but this does not prevent learning and creativity. They can still build on past experience, even though short-term memory plays tricks. Personal relationships are as important as ever, and contact with others—young and old—keeps folk mentally alert, encouraged, challenged. The death of partners, brothers and sisters can leave some elderly living as recluses. When this happens their sense of wellbeing decreases drastically; they lose a sense of self-worth and feel useless. People in this age group need affirming as much or more than anyone else. Churches can help a great deal here if they can involve them in various forms of service to others that help them to know they are still needed and have something to give to others.

Financially, life becomes harder. Pensions are limited, and inflation makes inroads. While a married man may enjoy a full occupational pension whether his wife lives or not, the woman is usually reduced to half of that pension if he dies; she faces years on the edge of poverty. There is still injustice and discrimination against women where pensions are concerned. And in this poverty they may need different housing, more heating, more medical help and transport, better food and home care.

The eighties show a marked change. Frailty and illness increase, and survival becomes the dominant concern of these people's lives. As friends die, grief and loneliness become the keynotes of many lives, and increasingly people in this age group must rely on others for the things they once did for themselves. This adds humiliation to other emotions. As long-time friends die, they turn back to past memories. The world around changes faster, but they cannot keep up; it becomes an unfamiliar place of fear and insecurity. The doctor is no longer available whenever needed, instead a stranger comes. The shops get too confusing; the cash desks are crowded and run by strangers; and even the milkman no longer delivers every day.

Spiritually, most people have deep needs that they cannot satisfy. Those who are old in the 1980s were conditioned to keep their own counsel and did not discuss their deepest feelings. Many have no real knowledge of God and nowhere to turn as they face the reality of death. Others have walked with God all their lives, and know that the one who died and rose again from the dead will give life to them also. But only the Lord has actually walked that way before and come back to prove he has conquered death. Paul describes death as the last enemy to be overcome (I Cor. 15:26). We are urged to 'encourage one another with these words' (I Thess. 4:18), but usually in our culture there is only a great silence. Jack Dominian comments: 'There is a need for withdrawal from the world to seek its Creator and Saviour, and these years encourage this.'

Raymond Bakke, in his recent book *The Urban Christian*, stresses the need to draw out and encourage the human resources that already exist in a group. Too many meetings still rely on the Victorian 'we the leaders' organising things for 'them'; and 'they' remain passive, uninvolved, unresponsive. Time for the very elderly almost stands still. The past has gone and the future barely exists. They must survive in the present as best they can.

If joyful memories and experiences from the past can be recalled, the present is made more significant and perhaps the future can be anticipated. If simple skills can be utilised, life in the present is once more meaningful and useful. Someone actually needs them, even if it is only washing coffee cups for the Mother and Toddler group, to set another person free. How far can we enable such people to use once more the resources they still possess? How much can we involve everyone in decisions made for the group?

Meetings?

How should the churches minister to these people, with their own special needs? Priority and time are given to the children, teenagers and families, and these are vital for the future, but the elderly get forgotten. Again and again in the Old Testament the Lord reminds his people of his special concern for widows, orphans, strangers in their land—the most vulnerable and defenceless groups in society, and from the beginning the Early Church was concerned for the widows among them. The main services and fellowship groups are vitally important, for 'God sets the lonely in families'. (Ps. 68:6) At its best the Church family is a place where they can remain in a community, in touch with all ages, with people around to help as necessary. Some churches have women's groups small enough to include everyone from mothers and toddlers to the elderly, and this can be a great blessing to all, as long as the noise is not too·great!

Most churches, however, have day-time meetings for the elderly on their own. These are usually for women, but there are some for men, and a few cater for both. Those for women tend to remain traditional, with a visiting speaker, a hymnbook familiar to a previous generation, a cup of tea, and a chat afterwards. The degree of loneliness is revealed when some attend two or three of these each week in different churches. Many of these groups are evangelistic, bringing together people who do not normally attend a church. Others concentrate on Bible Study, worship and prayer. But they all meet people's need for friendship and provide help and support where necessary.

However, this traditional style of meeting leaves problems. The older generation have sat and listened passively all their lives and have never had to be involved. Moreover when meetings are held after lunch, many find it hard to concentrate and feel sleepy. But it is pleasantly un-demanding, familiar, easy. One can sit comfortably through the same format every week and do nothing, while the message flows over one's head. Many people hate change and cling to the familiar. The deeper the rut, the better. It is not surprising that there is apparently little response to the Gospel.

Yet the Christian message is not one to be ignored. We have Good News, to be proclaimed to all, but the news demands a verdict, and everywhere the Lord went, people divided. Some believed in him, others rejected him.

Some have sat in traditional meetings for years and years and no one knows whether they have understood the message and responded or not. What is worse, they may not even know themselves. They may have unconsciously assi-milated elsewhere a mass of secular ideas and folklore in-compatible with the Christian message, but they have never expressed them even to themselves. They cling to the Authorised Version because they 'know it' and it is familiar, but they do not really understand the archaic language. After years of sitting in meetings, some may still find it difficult to read a Bible story to themselves. The leaders pour in hours of faithful loving service, and little is accomplished.

Setting Goals

The leaders of any meeting need to gather together once or twice a year to pray over the goals for the group for the coming months. Why is the group meeting? What is it trying to achieve for those who come? Who *does* come? What are their needs? The Bible describes the church as a building. (I Cor. 3:10 f.) Are we carefully laying foundations, building walls for a purpose? Or are we just throwing bricks in a heap on a building site, trying to fill a programme with any speaker we can get hold of? Some groups with new members may need to teach again the basic truths of the Gospel. Other groups who know these may need more emphasis on personal response and commitment to the

Lord. Others may need nurturing in the Christian life as they take their first steps.

The Engel scale can help us to determine these goals.[1] (See diagram on p. 197) Only God knows people's hearts, but the scale may help us in a general way to assess where people are, and where they need to move next. It is a challenging thought that most people will be between −6 and +2 on the scale, but there are thousands around us in the −8 to −10 group who never come near the church.

How Do People Learn?

We have a message to proclaim and teach, but we have not taught anything unless others have learned it. The Christian message demands a response. Certainly the Holy Spirit must open people's hearts to the truth, but God has chosen to proclaim his message through human teachers, and if our presentation clouds the message, it is harder for others to receive it.

How do people learn? Not so long ago only children 'learnt' in order to become adult and 'arrive'. Now we are recognising that people learn all through life, even in old age. The cyclic diagram on p. 198 illustrates what happens.

The one who hears the teaching must think about it, absorb it, accept it, act on it, and so—with the power of the Holy Spirit—change. But the present form of most meetings does not encourage thinking and acting. The message flows over people's heads year after year, without response.

Many churches are recognising this problem and restructuring their meetings for more participation from those who gather. Women's meetings have tried to involve people in crosswords, favourite verses and hymns etc. But we really need to go much further, to help people take in and respond to what they are hearing. Even when churches have made major changes in other meetings, those for the elderly have scarcely changed, and the leaders are left to struggle on as best they can.

The Engel Scale

This was drawn up originally by Dr James Engel, and is written up in *What's Gone Wrong With The Harvest?* by Engel and Norton (Zondervan 1975). It is a model of the spiritual decision-making process which commends itself as stating clearly what most Christian leaders know. It has been presented in several forms.

THE ENGEL SCALE

GOD'S ROLE	CHURCH'S ROLE		MAN'S RESPONSE
General Revelation		−10	Awareness of the supernatural
		−9	No effective knowledge of Christianity
Conviction	Presence	−8	Initial awareness of Christianity
		−7	Interest in Christianity
	Proclamation	−6	Awareness of basic facts of the Gospel
		−5	Grasp of implications of the Gospel
		−4	Positive attitude to the Gospel
	Persuasion	−3	Awareness of personal need
		−2	Challenge and decision to act
Regeneration		−1	Repentance and faith
A NEW DISCIPLE IS BORN			Matthew 28. 19–20
Sanctification		+1	Evaluation of decision
		+2	Initiation into the church
		+3	Become part of the process of making other disciples
		•	Growth in understanding of the faith
		•	Growth in Christian character
		•	Discovery and use of gifts
		•	Christian life-style
		•	Stewardship of resources
		•	Prayer
		•	Openness to others
		•	Effective sharing of faith and life

(Rejection)

Barriers to Learning

While those in their sixties can face some fresh challenges, and an active group can 'carry' older people more limited by age, change still raises barriers, and we need to understand these if we are to help people cross them. Fear is a major problem. People are afraid of revealing their ignorance, afraid of failing in public, afraid of embarrassment, afraid of anything new and different they may not be able to handle. They no longer have the resilience of youth. Past experiences may make them wary; concentration can vanish under stress. (One lady said she could not make sense of the healing at the pool of Bethesda until panic subsided; it 'began to make sense' the third time she read it. What are we achieving if our members have sat and listened for years and still cannot read the Bible for themselves?) People learn at different speeds: some slower, some faster. Some learn by seeing, some by hearing, or feeling. Some still remember easily, some do not. One group was annoyed when asked to

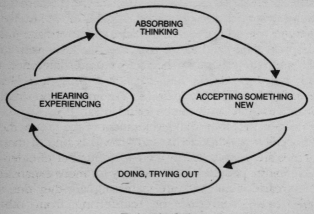

The Learning Cycle

write answers in exercise books—these women had not used them since leaving school 50 years before. Learning was for children. But they began, and their group was transformed by a whole new dimension in Bible Study alone and together. (And they were all over 60!)

All this means that change must be simple, non-threatening, and not too fast, but older people *can* change, and have joy in new achievements and discoveries. But sitting and listening is not enough. Variety helps concentration, and we all need to be encouraged to think about what we hear.

The meeting can start with the occasional buzz group for four or five minutes, when people can be asked to discuss something with their neighbours, in twos and threes—something they know a little about already. 'If someone asked you what God is like, what would you say?' or if that is too personal, 'What do some people think God is like?' Most people can contribute something, even one lady who confessed she hadn't a clue, and another who admitted she imagined God as an old man in a boiler suit, and knew as she said it how inadequate it was. If they can share their ideas with the speaker, they will probably listen better when she speaks on the subject because she is starting where they are, and they have already started thinking for themselves. Sometimes we do not realise the false ideas we have until we express them, and as we compare our ideas with the Bible, and with others, we begin to see the difference. If larger meetings divide into smaller groups, it is less threatening for all to take part. (An example of one simple approach to Bible study can be found in Part II.)

As leaders pray over the development of the group, they need to look at other areas, and growth is one of them. Churches are surrounded by a growing number of elderly, lonely, fearful, people. We should pray for more expansion and outreach. If numbers are increasing, are they due to people being converted, or transferring from other churches, or coming back to the Lord after turning away? Numbers are bound to decrease through death, but are others drifting away? If some leave because they resent changes, does it matter? If they resist change of all kinds, they may already have rejected the message, and it would be tragic if the resistance of one or two prevented the growth of the rest. Are people growing in serving each other? Are they growing in maturity and the knowledge of God? Are they growing in friendship, fellowship, relationship?

The diagram on p. 201 may help us assess the level of relationships in a group. Some function only at Level 1—the level of slight acquaintances meeting on the street exchanging greetings with 'Good Morning', 'How are you?'—a level where we expect standard answers, 'Very well, thank you'— and it is embarrassing if someone does launch into telling you how she really is. People do not really relate at this stage—words are a formality. On the other hand, at some meetings over a cup of tea, the local gossip and family stories of Level 2 can be exchanged and people get to know a little more about each other. At Level 3, people feel confident enough with their friends to share ideas and opinions, but many, especially the elderly, have never shared their deeper feelings outside the family, and now there may be few family left. As a result, they are starved at Level 4. Living alone means they have no one to share their fears, anxieties, affection, frustration, joy, despair, so these remain locked inside. They were brought up 'not to get involved', 'to keep themselves to themselves'. Even when they meet people, there is no communication about the things that matter most. Communication at Level 5 would come only between very close personal friends.

One of the greatest bridges between ourselves, others and God, is prayer. It helps to span the gulfs we create between us, and points people away from themselves to a loving Heavenly Father. Together we can acknowledge our dependence on him, and support each other as we bring our needs to him. We have no right to pry into the lives of others or violate the boundaries of privacy, but we do have a

Level 5	Absolute openness/honesty
Level 4	Feelings
Level 3	Ideas Opinions
Level 2	Gossip Stories
Level 1	Greetings

Levels of Relationship

responsibility to stand alongside and be there to support and encourage when needed.

Of course there are many who grow old surrounded by friends and family, still able to get about and live an interesting and fulfilled life. Old age can be a rewarding time, and is not necessarily difficult. Nevertheless the churches need to be aware of the elderly in their ministry, and Gary Collins in his book suggests a number of areas where they can help. There are several starting points for a concerned church.[2]

1. Plan specific programmes (some churches arrange holiday weeks with outings, meals, films etc).
2. Speak to the spiritual needs of the elderly including insecurity, insignificance, a sense of alienation from God, regret over past failure, fear of death.
3. Stimulate social and spiritual contact both with their own age and with the young.
4. Help meet physical and material needs (and we could add—see they receive what they are entitled to under

Social Security). Most of them are 'powerless' in society, and others must cope for them.

5. Visit them at home and in nursing homes etc.
6. Influence local and government programmes for the elderly by writing to the local MP and council.
7. Ensure the church building is physically accessible for them.
8. Create opportunities for older people to make a positive contribution to the church community in visiting, praying, helping with clerical and maintenance work, etc.

There are many older women in the churches already devoting hours of service to the elderly, but they need much more help and support. Serving one another is not very fashionable these days. It is more interesting to have fellowship with one's contemporaries instead. But much more could be done. How many churches provide warm, attractive, comfortable rooms and chairs to make the elderly feel welcome? How many supply large-print Bibles? Transport to and from meetings is a major problem for some. If the Lord cares for widows, so should we. He saw one putting all she had into the temple treasury; he had compassion on another whose only son had died; he healed a mother-in-law too ill to cope with a houseful of visitors.

The Church needs to stand up today on behalf of the aged and to work for just pensions, adequate heating allowances in extra cold weather, and the right amenities to give them as full a life as possible. 'He has showed you, O man, what is good. And what does the Lord require of you? To act justly and to love mercy and to walk humbly with your God.' (Mic. 6:8)

Valerie Griffiths

Note

[1]This scale is adapted from *What's Gone Wrong with the Harvest?* (Engel and Norton, Zondervan, 1975) by Roy Pointer in *Is My Church Worth Joining?* (Bible Society, 1982)

and used with permission.
[2]Adapted from Gary Collins, *Christian Counselling* (Word Publishing: 1987).

Valerie Griffiths worked as a missionary in Japan for 10 years with Overseas Missionary Fellowship (OMF) and 13 years in Singapore, where she saw one of her women's groups turn into a church. While on furlough, Valerie was active in speaking at women's meetings, especially among the elderly, seeing the need in many cases for radical change. She has since been involved on the Mission to London Women's committee, helping the leaders of women's groups. Valerie is married to Michael, who is Principal of London Bible College.

PART II

ONE TO ANOTHER

1. Introduction

While the stories in Part I all deal with specific groups of women, Part II looks at the whole nature of women's groups, with suggestions for them, old and new. It opens with a section on 'Sharing What Comes Naturally', emphasising the importance of friendship between women as a basis for communicating the Gospel. At the heart of most women's groups is a desire to share common experiences, anxieties and concerns; to give and receive mutual inspiration and support; to withdraw for a while from the demands of work (and in some cases family) in order to laugh, to cry and to pray.

Christian women's groups have an added responsibility to provide the kind of open environment where women who are not Christians can feel at home and find support. Where they are seen to be outward-looking and in touch with women's concerns in the wider world, they are more likely to be successful in communicating the Good News of the Gospel.

The articles in this section help look at some of these concerns. They include material on how to run a group, look at our understanding of God and at the kind of language we use. Examples of sketches about women and men are included which can be read formally or just for fun. There are also guidelines to help the sexually abused.

Finally, a list of women's organisations is included for those who wish to be linked with a specific group. It is not comprehensive, but a guide to show where the gaps still lie and where new initiatives are still needed. We have also added a list of selected books for those who wish to read further.

2. Sharing What Comes Naturally

It is a wonderful fact that at the heart of the Christian message is Good News for women: Everyone is special to God, so much so that he sent Jesus to live as one of us, and to die to break the power of sin and death, darkness and despair in our lives. As a result, women from all walks of life can now know life, hope, peace and joy in their daily experience. As we realise this afresh, it can help us to understand ourselves and others in a deeper way.

Understanding Ourselves

As women, we often view ourselves negatively and are easily diverted by feelings of inadequacy, low self-image, loneliness and self-pity. As we look at other women, we often take the positive things about them, from which we then make up a formula for the perfect Christian woman, wife and mother! This picture is always at the back of our minds, and we measure everything we do by its standard. What we forget is that there is no perfect woman—neither in the Bible, nor in the Church, nor in the nation, nor in the world. Very often, our low self-image comes from the fact that we don't accept ourselves as we are and cannot believe that anyone else can either.

Some years ago, I went through a stage when I tried to change myself. To those who know me, I am fairly extrovert and talkative. I became convinced that God could use quiet people much better than people like me, and they always seemed to have so much more grace! I decided I should become quiet. I tried this for three weeks! In the end, people thought I was 'off colour' and several asked me if I was all right. Through reading Psalm 139, I was reassured that God made me as I was, and that I was precious to him. Each of us is unique. I was trying to be someone God had not intended me to be.

Often we spend endless hours of agony and pre-occupation with our failures and self-image. This is not necessary, nor is it ultimately a good use of time! At the end of Psalm 139, the psalmist says 'Search me, O God, and know my heart; test me and know my anxious thoughts. See if there is any offensive way in me and lead me in the way everlasting.' To allow God to fulfil his purposes in our lives, there has to come a time when we allow him to search us from within: to come to a place of repentance and release us of those sins, fears and guilt feelings—which are all too familiar—in order to receive the cleansing and forgiveness that flow from Jesus himself. In coming to terms with ourselves as we are, we allow God further access to our lives. God can use all of us, whether we are noisy or quiet, fat or thin, introvert or extrovert. Most of all, he looks at the heart.

Thanking God for the way he has made us and offering ourselves to him in a fresh way enables us to receive his love and acceptance, which can then radiate to others. This does not mean that we have to go running, dancing, clapping and singing praise to the Lord in every situation! It does mean that as our hearts are turned to him, we desire to live for him and want to share him naturally with others, and then this becomes more and more possible. In Philippians 4:6, 7 we read, 'Do not be anxious about anything, but in everything, by prayer and petition, with thanksgiving, present your requests to God. And the peace of God, which transcends all understanding, will guard your hearts and your minds in Christ Jesus.' Many women will agree that this is important when it comes to our thinking processes—those trains of thought that can lift us up one minute, and lead us to the pit of despair the next. In spite of all the demands and preoccupations each day brings, women can experience a deep sense of God's peace and presence which helps to lead us through stress-filled days.

Those of us who have experienced peace in this way have something extremely valuable to share with other women. None of us can ultimately express with confidence what she has not experienced personally. Whatever our experience of knowing Jesus, the positive changes that have come as a result are powerful and can be naturally shared.

Making Contacts and Finding Friends

Central to the ministry of Jesus was friendship. He went out to people, talking and listening to them, praying with them and befriending them in a whole variety of different circumstances. This is how he can use you and me, as we learn to befriend women wherever they are.

Women normally find it easier to form friendships than men. Most women can relate to other women fairly easily, as the opportunity arises. We all recognise that the art of getting into conversations with others is not always easy at first, even though a friendship may develop later.

The process of moving from an opening conversation involves various stages. Everything should be a natural progression. Discover what common ground you have as people first. This can include anything from babies, children, work, the CND, books you have read or TV programmes you have seen, to similar interests, hobbies or life experiences.

I have recently formed a new friendship with a woman called Jane. After our initial conversation, we discovered that our husbands have similar jobs. Because of this, we struck up an understanding. It is important to remember, of course, that not every contact with someone will develop into a friendship. We must pray, asking the Lord to show us one or two people we can get to know. We will soon discover at what level it is appropriate to continue. There may be someone in our road, college, office or luncheon club, someone we met when we gave birth to our babies or who takes the same bus or train to work. For most of us, there are at least two or three women we see regularly, with whom we can begin to share the Good News of the Gospel.

How to Share What Comes Naturally

It always takes us by surprise when we have prayed for opportunities and they actually happen! At times like these, I always pray that the Lord will do for me what he did for Ezekiel: that he will stick my tongue to the roof of my mouth, and release it when he has given me the right words to say! (See Ezek. 3:26.)

Sharing what comes naturally involves sharing our experience and walk with God on a daily basis. In other words, what we tell others about does not only involve the experience of becoming a Christian but of going on as Christians. It is important not to allow personal pressure, striving and guilt to motivate our sharing. Being natural is the hallmark of good communication, even though it may take time. I remember being in a women's group a few years ago, and the conversation turned to church. One of the women turned to me and said, 'You go to church, don't you?' I prayed and perspired and said, 'Yes.' Then she asked me if I believed in God, and why. All I could say was, 'I know Jesus as Lord of my life, and he set me free to be myself because it says in his word, "If the Son shall set you free you shall be free indeed".' That was all I said. On the way home, I condemned myself and felt I had failed. But even that one answer—however inadequate I may have felt it was at the time—had an effect in this woman's life.

Sometimes we can say too much and detract from what may have been more appropriate in the situation. On other occasions, we will be given opportunities to say more than just a few sentences. God can use us as a link in a woman's life to draw her to Jesus when others have been involved in this process before us. If we think of our own conversions, for some of us, it was seeing the difference that Jesus made in the life of a close friend. Being prepared to be a link in the chain in what we say and do can bring us to a richer understanding of our own faith too. It releases us from the burden of feeling that unless we tell others about the whole Bible from cover to cover, then we have failed to convey the whole Gospel! Using the opportunities to share what God has done in our own lives in a whole host of different ways —how he answers prayer, for instance—can be just enough when talking to women individually. It is so easy to under-value the small things that happen to us. Yet if we look at the parable of the mustard seed, we read that something small grows into a great big plant (Matt. 13:32). We can trust God to make use of the small things we share with others, believ-ing that the work of his Spirit can do far more than we ever thought or imagined.

It is a relief to know that his word does not return to him empty, but accomplishes all that he desires (Isa. 55:11). Each of us has something to share. If we are sharing joys and sorrows, weaknesses and strengths with Christian friends, it becomes easier to share what God is doing in our lives with those who *aren't* Christians. Sadly there are times when, even as Christians, we don't share at this level with each other, because we are afraid of what others will think. But we need to encourage each other to get beyond this reti-cence and to reach out. We cannot share anything of value from a position of strength in ourselves (in fact when we're over-confident we're more likely to be insensitive), only from a place of weakness, giving God's Spirit room to fill us with his power and strength.

We can learn a great deal from the story of the Samaritan woman, who after her encounter with Jesus was filled with joy and ran home to tell others. We read that 'many of the Samaritans from that town believed in him because of her testimony' (John 4:1–26, 39–42). This can be the same with us, too. Finally, let us ask ourselves a question: Do we believe that our lives are in God's hands and can be strategic wherever we are? As we live in relationship with him, share his love, we are told that the light of Christ surrounds us wherever we are and whatever we do! (II Cor. 4:6)

Practical Ideas

1. It is a good idea to have at our fingertips a simple outline for sharing the Gospel with others. This can consist of 5 or 25 verses—whatever suits us best. It's easy to say to someone 'I know that Jesus died on the cross for me, it says in the Bible . . . and then spend the next five minutes feverishly looking for the verses we want! Find Scriptures that communicate God's love, the fact of sin, its effects, what Jesus accomplished on the cross and what it means to receive the Holy Spirit and live a new life. (See examples later on in this section.) These can be very useful. Learn them by heart.

    Take a concordance and do a Bible study on the love of God. Work through various verses, reading them in context, and write in a notebook what you discover. Learn them well, so that God can use them when you come to share his love with others.

2. We should use every opportunity to share what God has done in our daily lives with our Christian friends and encourage them to share in a similar way with us. To help us, we can keep an index file alphabetically with topics which are of general human interest. Then we can build up a series of quotes, statistics, stories and Bible verses that are relevant to each; look in the newspaper, in magazines and make brief notes from books that we read.

3. We should pray for those in whom we sense God at work, with other Christian friends; meet regularly to pray for them, possibly forming a prayer triplet group. Wonderful stories have yet to be told of what God can do through our praying and sharing.

Judi Richards

3. 'It Would be Nice to Believe, but the Stigma Would be Awful . . .'

Most women are honest enough to admit that in spite of all that they have experienced, both good and bad, there must be something more. The Bible describes this as a spiritual awareness that can never be satisfied outside a personal relationship with God our Creator. Many women feel that life has dealt them a hard and unfair package—very different from the romantic view of love and marriage, which they expected to fulfil their dreams! Yet whether married or unmarried, divorced or living alone it seems that the pressures of life and the pains involved in relationships soon bring most of us to our knees. At the same time, there are many who seem quite happy and content, yet who still need to be challenged with the life and claims of Jesus. If you have ever tried to share the Gospel with women before, you will know that certain objections keep recurring. In some cases, they are merely common human objections to becoming a Christian, but often they seem to be peculiar to women and the lives women lead.

Let us look at one of these responses: 'It would be nice to believe, but the stigma would be awful!' This was the first response made by a friend of mine called Carol. Her husband Stuart had become a Christian, and she admitted to telling her friends about it more than Stuart had himself. But she simply did not want to be associated with traditional churchgoers. 'I suppose I was testing their reaction,' she said. 'To see how they would respond and to see whether or not they would think we were completely mad and reject us.' To her surprise many of them did not reject her. One or two, in fact, expressed great interest, and said how envious they were and how interested they would be to talk more. All this helped tremendously, but Carol was still put off by the thought of having a newly religious spouse, with all the stigma that people attach to religious people today.

Churchgoing

Many of us come from a background where we were made to go to church. Memories of churchgoing are for many of us deadly, and did nothing but put us off any real understanding of what it means to be a Christian. This seems to be especially so in areas where the stigma of being 'religious' is associated with being respectable—and for the most part very middle class! There is nothing more disturbing to a real and sensitive conscience than the hypocrisy of going to church and appearing to support the status quo, when deep down we have no religious feelings at all. Many are only too aware that what is being said from the pulpit, week after week, has little or no relevance to our daily lives once we step outside the church building.

Likewise, childhood memories of having to dress and behave well, and having to sit for long periods listening to a male voice droning on, have done little to endear us towards real Christianity. Rather, these things may have made us want to break free and find their own way in the world rather than God's way (if, of course, he is there at all). The 'stigma'—or label—of being religious, then, is still deeply rooted in many women's experience. It is good to find out whether this is a problem for individual women we meet simply by asking them, 'Did you come from a Christian background?' The answer we get will make it pretty clear one way or the other, and we can take things from there.

Colourless Christianity

Ann, another friend, remembers how the stigma for her lay in the fact that Christianity seemed to be associated with being gaunt and drab. The messages preached seemed to say that she had to obliterate herself, deny herself anything that was colourful and exciting and which really expressed her personality. It's true that all too often churches have given the impression that Christianity is dull, boring and totally dissociated from the richness and beauty of this life. Perhaps the evangelical tradition has concentrated too much on the doctrine of redemption at the expense of knowing God as Creator. Yet both doctrines are central to our understanding of the God who has revealed himself clearly to us in the Bible. Many Christian women suffer from a denial of colour, laughter and creative self-expression that is a denial of life itself. When being religious is associated with running a race in which this very life is somehow negated, it is no wonder that women are embarrassed and even shy away from the 'stigma' that inevitably comes with it.

Another reason why Christianity at first seems so unattractive is that everything seems so formal when we first go to church. Somehow we feel we have to 'hold ourselves in' and exercise an amazing self-control just to get through a service that isn't immediately clear, nor relevant to life as we see it. The ability to juggle the various books and leaf through them to the right pages presumes that everyone who comes is both literate and familiar enough with liturgical language to make sense of it. For women especially, who generally favour freedom of communication, it's easy to find the service very restrictive, particularly when there is no space for informal or personal involvement.

Those of us who have been Christians for some time realise that patterns of Christian worship vary enormously and that some can become a great boost to faith where they are creative. But for new believers, the strangeness and stark formality of what we 'do' in church remains a mystery, even though it is repeated at least once a week!

Honesty

To women who fear the stigma of becoming a Christian, then, what do we say? Firstly, if we are honest, many of us have felt the same. The Church often does appear out-dated, and much of what goes on in church continues to be sadly irrelevant. Even so, things are changing. Perhaps you go to a church which is a place of real fellowship, life, worship, and support—somewhere you wouldn't feel ashamed of bringing anyone. Great—if this is the case. However, even in less positive surroundings, as faith becomes real, the desire to meet with others who share the same faith eventually outweighs issues of formality (as well as other negatives some associate with churchgoing). The desire to worship God together takes over.

The effects of the charismatic movement in practically every denomination have brought with them a freedom and renewal in worship, fellowship and ministry which express themselves in all kinds of new and often unpredictable ways. The revival of folk craft in some churches has enabled women to get together, not just to make kneelers for the pews, or to do flower arranging, but to be involved in creative banner making and other crafts which provide an important shared context for creativity, friendship and fellowship.

The Good News

There need be no stigma about being a Christian today. Our own personal story of knowing Jesus can help to break down walls of prejudice that remain in people's minds against the real Christian Gospel.

The stigma of following Jesus is very different from that of being 'religious', but for those who feel it is a stigma, help them read one of the gospels and encourage them to read about the life of Christ. To be sure, the conclusion we reach in the end can only be as C S Lewis once said, that Jesus was either mad, bad, or God. The cards we carry ultimately depend upon which conclusion we make.

The good news then is that Christianity is for non-religious people. So, where do we go from here? In his book *You Must Be Joking*, Michael Green states that the real issues are not so much to do with being a religious person, but asking questions like:

> Are you concerned about truth?
> Have you the courage of your convictions?
> Are you willing to take your stand with a minority group?
> Do you want to find fulfilment?
> Are you interested in your future?[1]

Becoming a Christian addresses each of these questions simply and clearly. Each of us must find her own way of answering them, so that in turn others who come into our lives can benefit.

Kathy Keay

Note

[1]Michael Green, *You Must Be Joking* (Hodder and Stoughton: 1976).

4. Communicating Life Issues

No matter how much we may want someone to become a Christian, only the Holy Spirit can ultimately work in a woman's heart and bring her to a point of forgiveness and faith. Many of us have grown up with all kinds of schemes and systems for winning people to Christ. These are not bad in themselves, but we all need to adapt them in order to share what comes naturally.

Discussion and Supper Parties

One of the ways in which we can communicate the love of God to others is through discussions, evangelistic Bible studies, questionnaires and supper parties. Many wonderful evenings have been spent in small groups, over a meal, where people have first got to know each other, then discussed a specific topic of general interest. One evening which I shall remember for a long time was spent with a group of women from different countries. After hearing about their families over the meal, and having a generally relaxed, enjoyable time, we all sat on the floor with coffee, and I introduced the topic 'What is the most important thing in life?' There was a long pause. I then asked Josie from India to get the ball rolling. She replied, 'The most important thing in life is to love and to be loved.' In different ways each person in the room confirmed that they felt the same. Everyone mentioned something slightly different: the joy of meeting someone new; the irresistible attraction that often follows; the vulnerabilities involved in getting to know someone; the pain that comes from loving. No one had mentioned God at all, but there was a tremendous bond between everyone in the room. Each woman felt it. I suggested that this was because we had touched on the very nature of God, and communicated it between ourselves, possibly without realising it. We then went on to see (from the Bible) how the God whom Christians believe in is a God of love, one who can be understood most perfectly through the person of Jesus. Different people recounted different experiences of what it had meant to them to love and be in relationships which were painful because of love.

This concern is obviously paramount in most women's lives, and an understanding of how to communicate the love of God is worth working at, however you feel you can best communicate it.

How To Give a Talk

Try writing an outline for a talk you would like to give. Here is an example.

Theme: What is the most important thing in life for you?

Suggestion: The covenant love of God—the meaning of the rainbow.

Quote: 'I found it frightening that one could acquire everything one wanted and still be so miserable.' Actress Raquel Welch, or 'The only place we will ever be free of love's pain is hell.' C.S. Lewis.

Introduction: Against the background of meaninglessness, broken relationships, increased unemployment and the threat of a nuclear holocaust, many people are asking, What's it all about? Is there a God? Has he given up on us, or can we be confident that he will hear us if we call out to him? If he is there, will he deliver us from what often seem impossible circumstances, and give us a solid reason to hope for the future?

Visual aid: Make or buy a large rainbow, to be placed where everyone can see it at the beginning of the talk.

God's Promises

Explain that the Bible is a collection of books which record historic accounts of a God who has committed himself absolutely and for all time to those who put their trust in him. From the calling of Abraham and Sarah in Genesis 12 to the day when Jesus will come again, God's character is totally bound up with bringing life where there is none, hope where there is despair, and all that Jesus proclaims he himself has come to bring in Isaiah 61:1–3. The Good News for women today is that those who know Jesus personally continue his mission in the world; God wants women to bring Good News to the poor; bind up the broken hearted; proclaim freedom for the captives and release for the prisoners; to comfort all who mourn and to provide for those who grieve—to bestow on them a crown of beauty instead of ashes, the oil of gladness instead of mourning, and a garment of praise instead of a spirit of despair, so that all who respond to him will be called oaks of righteousness, a planting of the Lord for the display of his splendour.

There is no task that could be greater than this for any woman. Whatever our view of women's ministry in the official sense, every woman who loves Jesus has a lifelong assignment from him to learn how to continue his creative work in the lives of others.

God Knows Our Circumstances

Read Exodus 3:7 where God speaks to Moses. He declares 'I have indeed seen the misery of my people in Egypt. I have heard them crying out because of their slave drivers, and I am concerned about their suffering. So I have come down to rescue them from the hand of the Egyptians and to bring them up out of that land into a good and spacious land.' It has been the experience of many Christians that God has been as real in their circumstances as he was for the children of Israel. This includes women, especially those who suffer from broken relationships. The covenant love of God in these circumstances can become all the more powerful and relevant.

Why Has it Happened to Me?

All of us have no doubt asked this question at some point or another, especially if we are women who feel the struggle of life at times too much to bear. We may well ask why do we find ourselves in demanding and often impossible situations? Crises do occur; is it just a 'cop out' to reach out to God and ask him to take us in when times get hard? Is God only a crutch? In crises it is easy to fluctuate from feelings of self-pity to resolute independence. I know many women who feel they can't manage alone, yet at the same time are determined not to ask for help from others. Married and single women alike often 'live lives of quiet desperation', waiting for someone to break through and bail them out. This may or may not be realistic. However, it does help to know more broadly why crises occur, and to be able to understand (at least partly) reasons for suffering in the world in which we live.

In his book *The Cost of Commitment*, John White shows that suffering is the common lot of humanity. He states that we are all part of a fallen world—a world spoiled by human selfishness deeply rooted in every area of life. We suffer from our own sins and stupidities. We need to accept that we will never be fully free from the effects of sin, and at times choose courses of action that are unhelpful, even detrimental to our ultimate good. Also, we suffer from outward afflictions—those events and tragedies which come upon us and in which we are often at our most powerless. Almost every woman will have some incident in her life of this kind. For many women, experiences of bitterness and hopelessness have been met by the sisterhood of the feminist movement which has helped to give them new momentum and a reason for living. However, afflictions from outside often occur when we are most alone, and women from all backgrounds need to know how to react in tough situations in order to prevent them getting even more hurt.

What the Bible Says

The Bible is full of accounts by people who called on God in their troubles and who were helped, though not always instantly. It is good to become familiar with stories of women in the Bible like Sarah, and Esther and Hannah; Ruth, Mary, Martha and Elizabeth. Ruth offers one of the best and perhaps the most celebrated examples of a woman who had found favour and security in God. Mary's story (Luke 1:46–55) invites other women to find their way to Jesus, the true liberator and Lord.

Deliverance

David's testimony could be repeated hundreds of times by women throughout the centuries who have experienced God's redemptive love in their lives (II Sam. 22:2). 'The Lord is my rock, my fortress and my deliverer.' He delivers people from overwhelming troubles, fears and on occasions even death itself (Ps. 56:13).

It is good to remind ourselves of his promises. 'Even to your old age I am he. I will carry you, I have made and I will bear you.' The good news here is that we can be in relationship with a God who will move us through difficult and often traumatic circumstances time after time on our journey, until we eventually see him face to face.

This is echoed by the New Testament writers who state 'He has delivered us from such a deadly peril, and he will deliver us. On him we have set our hope that he will continue to deliver us. (II Cor. 1:10)

God's activity on our behalf is continuous, involving the past, present and future. The delivery is not usually instant. Rather like the birth of a baby, it is often a long and painful process which has to be gone through. In other words, coming to know Jesus does not always protect us from life's difficulties. Rather we have his assurance that he will be with us, and bring us through, no matter what our circumstances. 'The Lord will rescue me from every evil attack and will bring me safely to his heavenly kingdom.' (II Tim. 4:18)

Women with broken relationships, health problems, a sense of meaninglessness in work, a longing for something beyond the present, may wish to see instant change. Deliverance may involve God changing our circumstances—for example in physical healing, or through provision of money, when needed, through others. Alternatively, and more usually, he will enable us to come through life's various experiences positively, even though circumstances do not change.

At this point in the talk we can have a time for open questions and comments.

Making Sense of It All

A talk such as this shows that sharing the Good News of the Gospel with women therefore involves much more than helping them to understand what it means to become a Christian. For almost every woman, sooner or later, it means coming to terms with the burdens which each bears—big and small—in her daily life: the demands and anxieties of children, singleness, living with a violent husband, looking after sick and elderly relatives, knowing what to do about financial worries, coping with sudden news of bereavement or redundancy. Just as he did with Job, Satan wrestles with each of us, as we face a whole variety of different and difficult situations, in order to make us lose faith and to doubt the covenant love of God. But there is no situation which the love and presence of Christ cannot enter and eventually transform.

The story of our lives consists of times when we can experience a more direct and immediate contact with God, as well as those when he seems to be absent, and apparently leaves us struggling. In both cases, however, the point to emphasise is that he is with us, redeeming (ie recreating) all that would potentially harm us. Jesus has committed himself to our ultimate good.

Encourage Bible Reading

Through reading the Bible we discover what God is like, so that we can recognise him at work in others. 'A man of sorrows, and familiar with suffering.' (Isa. 53:3) 'For we do not have a high priest who is unable to sympathise with our weaknesses, but we have one who has been tempted in every way, just as we are—yet was without sin.' (Heb. 4:15) When we are tempted to go our own way rather than God's way, we can remember that Jesus went through similar temptations and is wonderfully able to help us. 'Although he was a son, he learned obedience from what he suffered.' (Heb. 5:8)

Whatever our own personal battles, the covenant love of God can hold us fast, so that we can say to one another with confidence, 'we know one who sticks closer than a mother.'

Kathy Keay

5. How to Run a Lunch and Dinner Club

For those inspired by the chapter in Part I entitled 'Christian Viewpoint—Christian Lunch and Dinner Clubs', there are many practical points to consider before arranging your first meeting.

Prayer must be priority. Usually a small group of women form a main planning group. Their activities will include:

1. individual and collective prayer;
2. providing guidance for a larger working group;
3. planning a suitable programme for your area (this may include reviewing past events and looking ahead at requests which need to be shared and prayed for);
4. printing clear programmes for invited guests with topical titles and clear details of dates, times, venue and speaker.

Hosting

It is important that at least one or two people care for the guests before, during and after each event. These should be committed Christians with a vision for the work, willing to get involved in the events. They must be able to share with their guests an active and meaningful faith in appropriate ways, and willing to follow up relationships in their homes and churches, with counselling where necessary.

Tickets

Tickets should be issued to the hosts and hostesses at the

first planning meeting, giving plenty of time for careful distribution. All details should be clearly marked; the hostess's name can also be written on the ticket. Then, each hostess can commit herself to distributing a certain number of tickets as appropriate. Naturally, in different locations seating arrangements will vary. The ideal situation is to have one hostess in charge of each table with about eight guests. The tables should be numbered and the hostess's name clearly seen. An attractive table arrangement is obviously important, and place names are often helpful.

Another practical part of the paperwork preparation is allocating someone to look after a book table and to keep accounts.

Venue

The venue will vary in each area, but here are some factors to take into consideration: Do you have the people and facilities to do your own catering—a large home or church premises? Are you in an area where neighbours and friends are used to eating out? Are your guests more at home on neutral ground rather than church premises, at a home, hotel or community centre?

If you decide to use commercial premises, can you choose a suitable hotel or restaurant which is easily accessible, and can you negotiate reasonable terms with the management with regard to the price of the meal? How long before the meal may you have access to the room? Do you require the bar to be open? Good relationships with the staff are important when booking any venue. Is there a facility for recording the speaker, if he or she permits this?

Speaker and subject

Through the speaker, singer or special feature, discussion and questions can be stimulated both during and after the meal. The planning group should decide well in advance what kind of programme members want.

Someone should be allocated the task of inviting speakers in good time in a clear letter including date, time, venue and duration of meeting, suggesting the title of the talk, and indicating the aims and size of the event. A reminder letter should be sent two weeks before the event, repeating the details and giving clear instructions as to how to reach the venue. Overnight accommodation should be offered if the speaker is travelling from a distance, and any gift for travel, time and effort should be realistic—sent before the event if possible.

In addition, some clubs find it helpful to use a feature—a soloist, a practical demonstration, or book reviews—before the meal and speaker. This helps relax guests, attracts attention and breaks the ice.

Finance

There are two main views on financing lunch and dinner clubs, and it is important to decide which view your group is to take, so that everyone knows where she stands. Some believe that the price of tickets takes into account the meal, printing, speaker's expenses, postage, flowers, hire of premises, etc—in other words, all overheads. Others are convinced that the price of the ticket should cover only the meal, and all other expenses are met by voluntary Christian giving. Decide in advance!

Follow up

In the end, it will be the little things that matter and that make the dinner run smoothly. Hence, make sure there is free literature available (eg gospels, and booklets on how to become a Christian). Good suggestions are *Knowing God Personally* (Campus Crusade for Christ) or *Journey into life* (Falcon). Also, make sure there is somewhere available to talk to people who want to speak in confidence.

6. Guidelines for Women's Groups

Many women's groups are out of date, need fresh blood, or presume that all women have the same agenda. Perhaps we do—why not find out? There is certainly room to start a new kind of women's group in most churches today.

Why Start a Women's Group?

Women's groups aim to enable women to work through issues relating to women at a local level, preferably within a local church context, to bring about wholeness in the lives of those concerned and the ability to help others.

Subjects for discussion may well come from the group itself. These will differ according to who is in the group; what part of the country you are from (because of differing attitudes in rural and urban communities); the number of women in the group; and the issues facing single people, married, single parent and divorcees within the group. Suggestions within this chapter are merely those that may be useful when a group doesn't have its own agenda.

Basic to any group should be the desire to establish a biblical perspective on issues relating to women—seeking to understand what the Bible says and its relevance in our lives today. This doesn't mean, however, getting stuck on issues of headship and the more difficult Pauline passages. Women's groups should also aim to encourage discussion and mutual support about concerns such as work, birth, death, home, sexuality, health, education, etc, where female comment is both important and often left out within church groups.

Getting Started

Common objections to starting a group will be raised. Here are a few that may be familiar to you:

> I'm not a gifted speaker
>   or a religious fanatic
>   or an organisational genius
>   or someone with lots of spare time
>   or a strong Christian with *all* the answers (thank goodness!)

If you can overcome these hurdles, you'll need only one or two people to get something going, somewhere to meet (preferably a home), a suitable time that doesn't clash with church meetings and family commitments, and someone to publicise an initial open meeting through the church and among friends. Aim to make full use of the church notice-board, church magazine, and telephone; to produce a duplicated circular to be distributed through the church and to whomever is interested by post or by hand. Send material to suitable contacts in the churches in your area as well. (In time this may lead to formation of different groups for different functions which can be church-based.)

Pitfalls and Potential

Groups often run into difficulty because there is too great a mix of people wanting to do things from a different basis. It may help to decide before sending out initial invitations what kind of group you want it to be: church-based or inter-church-based? For Christians only, or others too? For women only or women *and* men? Will it be organised or not? (That is, will there be a long-term programme eventually, or will it be planned from meeting to meeting?) Will it be predominantly feminist or for married women with children, or will it be for a wide range of women?

There may be room for specific meetings to invite specific groups. You may, however, prefer to have a mixed meeting to discover who is interested, then to make use of different ideological and Christian perspectives as the weeks go by.

Approaching the Church Leaders

One of the aims of a women's group should be to influence the Church in its structures and attitudes between men and women. Local groups where possible are encouraged to function through the local church. It is therefore a good idea to try to arrange an initial meeting with the church leaders to explain the aims of the group.

It is important to emphasise that a women's group is not in competition with other church groups, although what is discussed and implemented does have implications for the Church as a whole. Encourage your church leaders to give you the church's backing in this. Aim to keep communication lines open. This can be a major way of educating the church leaders and is worth plugging.

What If They Disapprove?

There is no reason why you should not start a women's group in your home, even without the backing of your church leaders. As long as this is done discreetly and doesn't clash with other commitments within the church, go ahead. But do aim to establish good relationships with your church leaders if you haven't already managed to; perhaps invite them to join you for a meal.

In conversation with church leaders you may suggest the possibility of sermons on women's issues—lend books, tapes, etc. Know what's on offer, and make sure the church does too. Offer to do book reviews and generally to raise the awareness of women's issues and activities within your church.

Emphasise that the women's group is *not* a threat to home and family; is not trying to push any particular line on women's ministry. On the other hand, we mustn't bury our heads in the sand. We need to point out the extent of influence from the women's movement within society, and the need to work through issues from a Christian perspective.

Going on in Prayer

Individuals may need and want personal support during any of life's critical moments. Prayer support groups and partnerships can develop between two or three people who become committed to pray for each other, especially after a bereavement, during pregnancy, when moving house, in the midst of difficult relationships, through health problems or any other difficult times.

This is an option, however, and should not be forced. Some members of the group may find it quite natural to link up in this way, while others need or prefer a different approach.

How Often and How Long?

After the initial meeting, each group should decide for itself how often to meet. Options could include once a month, once every two weeks or whatever is suitable. This will depend largely on the distance people have to travel and their own personal commitments.

Groups are likely to last only as long as the momentum is there to keep them alive. A commitment to good planning and supporting each member of the group (by drawing out their own personal needs and working on them over a period of time) can help avoid premature dispersal of a group. Ideas and questions among the group along with those that arise spontaneously from reading magazines, books, and newspapers will provide material for discussion and motivation for action.

Who Might Serve as a Resource?

If you wish to invite a speaker, consider anyone from among the following categories: women working in a male-dominated area; a local women's health worker; a local or national politician; a woman journalist or broadcaster; a deaconess or woman minister.

Keeping the Record

It is an advantage for someone to keep a record of what has been discussed at each meeting, points that have emerged and any particular issue which could provide for future meetings. Though this is not vital it can include suggestions which may spark off discussions on particular themes, books to read, review and comment on, and ideas to implant within the community to help people in need. Among any group even as small as only six members, there is almost always someone who enjoys careful record keeping.

How To Run a Small Group: A Basic Pattern

It makes a great difference if the leader is there early, welcoming people on arrival. Making people feel at ease helps create a positive atmosphere right from the start. This is only one of several guidelines, however, for a worthwhile meeting. Other suggestions are:

1. Begin promptly.
2. Ask each person to introduce herself, especially if there are any newcomers.
3. It may or may not be appropriate to open the meeting in prayer. The main thing is to be flexible and not to force things.
4. Introduce the purpose of the meeting. If there is a specific issue to be discussed, mention any papers/articles to be used as discussion material. If possible, duplicate material in advance, so that people have access to it during the meeting.

1. The Monologue

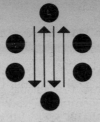

2. The Cosy Dialogue

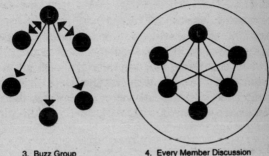

3. Buzz Group

4. Every Member Discussion

Types of Group Discussion

5. Encourage everybody to contribute (see suggestions on types of group discussion below). Avoid a monologue, unless you have deliberately asked someone to address the group. Interaction in the group should ideally be represented by type 4 in the diagram above, but this requires both leader and members to accept responsibility. All too often one of the other types prevails.

6. Leave time for people to share briefly what they have gained from the meeting. It is better if this is spontaneous. It should also allow for comments that need clarification or issues that have emerged and can be discussed next time.

7. Pray together if appropriate. The summary can lead very

naturally into a time of prayer if people are used to praying informally. If individuals want specific prayer and support in difficult situations, it is best to see how the group can help in practical ways. As trust grows, people usually become more committed to each other and offer support more naturally. But at first they may prefer to pray in smaller groups. When the group consists mainly of people who don't know each other, it may be more appropriate to end with a short period of silent meditation.

Suggestions for Group Discussion Topics

The following topics are equally relevant to men and women and may provide a helpful stimulus for anyone wishing to discuss them within the local church. For the purposes of this book, they are offered specifically for those who wish to start a local women's group. In all cases stimulating discussion starters are often available in the form of relevant leaflets or books.

Home

The practical outcome of roles in marriage: reasons for violence in the home; conflict between women's career and children; headship and its practical effects; divorce; remarriage; single parents; childrearing; motherhood and adoption; caring for elderly relatives; dependant people; home and family life; hospitality.

Relationships

Issues facing men and women alone; sexuality; lesbianism; the maternal single woman; God's expectations for husbands; marriage to a non-Christian partner; relationships between men and women; women and sex; marriage problems; loneliness; wholeness in relationships; childlessness; infertility.

Church

The need for the Church to change its attitude to single people; the feminist case against the church; unemployment and the Church; exploring the difficult Bible passages relating to women in the Church; tackling prejudice in authoritarian churches; how to gain the understanding of church leaders; sexist language in the Church.

Ministry

Women's ministry to men; theological training for women (a need to change the system?); women's contribution within politics; submission and leadership between men and women; women and leaders; women as peacemakers; can women teach men?

Health and Well-being

Women and mental health; how to deal with guilt; developing a Christian mind; depression; how to deal with low self-esteem; genetic engineering; self-acceptance.

General Topics

Coping with ambition and career; Christian women in the professions; biblical definitions of liberation and how to put them into practice; women's movements historically and the relevance to us today; education (is educating girls as necessary as educating boys?); women in advertising—do the media stereotype women/men?; feminists and spirituality; differences between men and women; creativity; liberation of men; how Christian men view feminism; how to change without being radical or without being dismissed; androgyny.

Application

Health Find out what special health facilities are available for women in your area. Do doctors give enough attention to gynaecological or emotional problems? Are the special needs of ethnic minority women cared for? What action might your group take to improve facilities? Bible passage: Luke 8:42b–48.

Race/class What special insights might working-class and black women offer on the Christian life? Are churches hearing their voices adequately? Find out if any women in the group feel excluded by the dominant culture in their church. What moves could be made to remedy this? Bible passages: Exodus 22:21–24; Leviticus 19:9–10; Ruth 2:1–12; Ephesians 2:16–19.

Politics Are women adequately represented in political life? If not, what differences might it make if they were? What part do women play in local politics in your area? Is anyone in the group actively involved? What difficulties does being in a minority in political life present? Bible passage: Luke 1:46–53.

Media Bring pictures from magazines, including adverts. What do they say about society's view of women and men? How do you feel about the people portrayed in TV drama? Are their lives anything like yours? How can we counteract false images? Bible passages: John 8:31–32; Philippians 4:8.

Church What is the 'profile' of women in your church? Are they steered into work amongst women and children, or behind the scenes? Ten per cent of the Bible deals with women's stories—do five sermons a year focus on this material? Are great Christian women of the past remembered enough? Bible passages: Judges 6:4–8; II Chronicles 34:22–24; Philippians 4:2–3.

Marriage What is meant by headship in marriage? If it is interpreted as 'authority', what does this mean in practice? How should Christians react to the widespread physical and mental abuse within marriages? Bible passages: Mark 10:1–9; Ephesians 5:21–33 (*not* just 21–24!)

Singleness Should marriage be every woman's goal? What attitude should single Christian women take to their singleness? What place is there for single women in the churches? Bible passages: Matthew 19:10–12 (especially GNB); I Corinthians 7:1, 8.

Home Married couples: keep a diary for a week of who does which domestic tasks (and time spent). Bring it to the group to discuss (put all the accounts in a hat and read anonymously!). Is work fairly shared? How is it divided—by ability, or by gender? Bible passages: John 13:1–5, 12–15; John 21:7–13 especially v 9.

Children Who spends most time with them—mother or father? Are childrearing tasks divided by gender (eg father disciplines, mother comforts)? Are boys and girls treated differently, channelled into different interests? Are they given the same amount of attention? Bible passages: Matthew 18:1–6, 10; Ephesians 6:1–4.

Childlessness Is childbearing the supreme experience of being a woman? What is church like for the childless? Biblical material: look up 'barren' or childless in a concordance. What impression do you get of the Bible's attitude?

Sexuality Many women are sexually abused in minor or major ways. What does this tell us about attitudes to male and female sexuality? What do you feel about women taking sexual initiative, or talking about sexual feelings? Bible passages: Genesis 2:25 (especially GNB); Song of Songs 5:2–16; II Samuel 13: 1–22.

Education Borrow some primary and secondary school textbooks from children. What images of men and women do they portray? Are girls and boys given different opportunities in education, or encouraged to pursue different careers? What do teachers and parents in the group feel about promoting equality in schools? Bible passages: Proverbs 4:5–9; Luke 10:38–42.

Work How important do women in the group feel work is to them? Is there 'men's work' and 'women's work'? Share any experiences of difficulty getting training or promotion; difficulty balancing work with other demands; sexual harassment at work. Is legislation against discrimination useful? Bible passages: Proverbs 31; Acts 9:36–39; Acts 16:14–15.

7. What is Male? What is Female?

A Group Activity

First, let each member of the group complete the question-naire below (or use an overhead projector). Let the members of the group discuss their responses. It is advisable to appoint a sensitive leader, so that everyone can hear and be heard.

Questionnaire

A Consider the following qualities. Do you think of them as belonging mostly to women or to men? Answer spontaneously, putting W for women or M for men beside each one:

gentleness	brilliance	self-esteem
strength	wit	loyalty
cleverness	charm	understanding
care	beauty	love
studiousness	leadership	pity
brashness	tenacity	self-denigration
fickleness	endurance	

B 1. Read the following story:

A father and son were travelling by car on an outing that took them across a railway level-crossing. Alas, the car stalled on the crossing and, despite desperate efforts, the ignition key stuck and the car refused to move before a train came and smashed into the car. The father was killed instantly but the boy was rushed to hospital and prepared for an emergency operation. But on entering the theatre, the surgeon took one look at the boy on the table and said, 'I cannot perform this operation. That boy is my son.'

How do you explain the surgeon's reaction?

2. Who, mostly, does these jobs? Again, answer spontaneously, writing W or M.

doctor	refuse collector	steeplejack
nurse	minister of religion	chief constable
gardener	cleaner	social worker
engineer	milk deliverer	army chief-of-staff
lawyer	road mender	bank clerk
au pair	TV Programe	supermarket
dentist	producer	manager
astronaut		

C Who does these jobs in your home? Quick answers again W or M—or other answers if, for example, your experience is of single sex households:

looking after children	paying bills
cleaning	mending broken machinery, etc.
cooking	
making beds	answering the door
washing	answering the telephone
ironing	dealing with canvassers
gardening	decorating rooms
putting things away	arranging holidays
knowing where to find things	rearranging furniture
sewing	buying clothes
	taking charge of finances

D Social behaviour: Imagine you are out for the evening with someone of the opposite sex, and you meet other men and women. Answer W or M:

Who orders the drinks?	Who does the introductions?
Who laughs loudly?	Who talks about clothes?
Who pays the bill?	children?
	food?

E Do you ever use the following expressions? Answer

truthfully, YES or NO.

lady doctor	helping wife or mum to wash up
girl (of a woman)	
my husband thinks . . .	thanking the ladies for making the tea
I wouldn't let my wife do that	

F What do you feel about expressing emotions of love, grief, anger, etc? Think carefully about this one, then answer in one or two sentences.

Double-sided Debate

For every woman that is:	*There is a man:*
Tired of being a weak person when she knows she is strong	Tired of looking strong when he feels vulnerable.
Tired of looking foolish	Tired of people expecting him to know everything.
Tired of being called an emotional female	Tired of the denial of the right to cry and be tender.
Tired of being used as a sexual object	Tired of being concerned about his virility.
Tired of being called not feminine because she is competitive	Tired of competing as the only way to prove his masculinity.
Tired of being tied to her children	Tired of being denied the pleasure of paternity.
Tired of being denied a satisfying job or a fair salary	Tired of being responsible for the economic situation of another human being.
Tired of being denied training in the mechanical details of her car	Tired of not being trained in the joy of knowing how to cook.
Who has ventured a step towards her own liberation	Who realises that the way to freedom has become easier.

'Women's Lib is also about Men's lib.'
     Does the group agree?

Language

Women both inside and outside the Church are becoming more sensitive to the prevalence of masculine terms in the language we use. In a gender-conscious age like ours, the Church cannot afford to be naive about such issues. Consider the following:

Example	Alternative	Comment
Man/men/mankind	people/persons/ humanity/human-kind/human beings/men and women/women and men/ every-one/all of us/we/ folk/friends	Generic term 'man' may refer to all persons or only to adult males. It may have the effect of excluding women from our language.
common man/ layman brothers/brother-hood/brethren/ fraternal	the average person/ordinary people/layperson/ laity/community/ kindred sisters and brothers/fellow-ship/brothers and sisters	Choice depends on context.
From 'Longing of the Heart' (Paul Carnes) 'To that longing which makes men turn toward one another in love rather than in estrangement, let us pray'	'To that longing which makes us turn toward one another in love rather than turning away in estrangemet, let us pray'	First person pronoun includes all.
From Views of God: 'Although they believe that God is spiritual in	'Although they believe that God is spiritual in nature and more than	Use 'human' instead of 'man'.

nature and more than man, they use physical and personal terms in speaking of him.'

human, they use physical and personal terms in speaking of God'

'Each child should have an opportunity to respond in his own way.'

'Each child should have an opportunity to respond in her or his own way'
'Children should have an opportunity to respond in their own way'

Satisfactory except for repeated use of 'his or her'. The second option is preferable because plurals do not distinguish the sexes.

What Do I Call Someone?

Dear Sir/Mr/Miss/ Ms/Mrs/He/She

Dear Sir or Madam
Dear Friend
Dear . . .
Dear Officer

Be as specific as possible. Use the title the individual prefers. Name the addressee or the office held. Second person does not distinguish the sexes.

postman/woman minister/poetess actress/chairman

postal worker
minister/poet/ actor
chair/chairperson
moderator/co- ordinator

Gender difference unnecessary. Many alternatives possible.

'The committee is headed by three Christians: Mrs Richard Jones (wife of a Christian minister), Mrs Emily Smith & John T. Brown.'

'They are: Susan M. Jones, Emily K. Smith & John T. Brown'

Use parallel terms to describe women and men.

Language Which Defines or Judges Women or Reinforces Stereotypes

men and women/ boys and girls	women and men/ girls and boys	Vary the order. Use plural or use specifically correct gender.
The Sunday School teacher . . . she	The Sunday School teachers . . . they	
'The ladies served coffee after church'	Mary Robinson and Harriet Moore served coffee . . .	Be specific.
'Ministers' wives were also present'	'Ministers' spouses were also present'	Women as well as men are ministers.
'Two pretty girls, dressed in their summer finery, lit the candles, while the boys handed out the programmes'	'Two girls lit the candles while the boys handed out programmes' 'The children lit the candles and handed out the programmes'	Use parallel terms or avoid describing tasks in terms of gender.

Note for Clergy of the Church of England

At present, no official guidelines exist for clergy wishing to avoid sexist language in liturgy. It is generally accepted that many alter the language (ie 'all people' instead of 'all men').

If you wish to make representation of behalf of your church/churches in your area, write to: Secretary General, Church House, Dean's Yard, London SW1.

8. The Gender of God: Beyond Male & Female

What is God like? Is 'he' male or female? Sooner or later someone is going to ask you.

Discussion

1 Try reading some passages from the Bible with the gender of God reversed, substituting 'she' and 'her' for 'he' and 'his', 'Queen' for 'King', and perhaps 'Lady' or 'Mother' for 'Lord'. You could try your own favourite passages, or some of the following: Exodus 15:1–7; I Samuel 2:1–10; Psalms 24, 34, 40, 111, 147; Ezekiel 30:20–26; Romans 3:21–31; I John 4:8–16.

   How did you feel when reading them? Why? Was there any difference between your feelings about the warlike and judgemental aspects of God and your feelings about the caring aspects? Did the gender reversal make any difference to your response to God's activity? Were you at all confused when trying to distinguish between 'he' meaning 'God' and 'he' referring to a person?

2 Is the gender of God important? Why?

3 God is not male; he is spirit. What do you think about this statement?

   Have you noticed its inconsistency?

Why Worry About the Gender of God?

Most Christians would define God in personal terms, addressing God as Father. However, is the language of prayer often descriptive (saying God is like a father), rather than definitive (say God is literally our father)? Perhaps your reactions to the discussion will have given you some ideas about why our image of God is important.

One reason why some people are worried by an exclusively male concept of God is that it seems to set a higher value on maleness than on femaleness. It is used as a reason for banning women from the priesthood, and for justifying the dominance of men over women in society generally, especially in positions of power.

We have deeply ingrained feelings about what is appropriate when talking about God. It is still virtually unthinkable for us to refer to God as mother rather than father, and it still seems odd to most of us. But if we believe that God is spirit, neither male nor female, or perhaps including and transcending both female and male, we *ought* to be free to use a variety of images. To limit our idea of God to maleness may well be considered idolatry because it restricts our picture of God to one particular aspect of divinity, to the exclusion of other female images outlined in the Bible.

The Bible and God

Most of our ideas and images of what God is like come originally from the Bible. The books of the Bible were written by men, as distinct from women, and the authors generally understood society, and God's action within it, in terms of their own structure. While the Bible clearly portrays women in crucial roles, the writers concentrated on the role of men in public life.

Women and women's experience were less significant. It is not possible to undo this balance towards male perspective because most of the female wisdom was not recorded and so has been lost. It is important instead to try to look freshly at scripture from a woman's perspective.

You could try doing this for yourself. As a start, look at the story of the crucifixion through the eyes of Jesus's women followers. Read the account in Luke 23:26 to 24:11. Notice, 'Great numbers of people followed, many women among them ... the women who had accompanied him from Galilee stood ... and watched it all.' They followed the body and 'took note of the tomb and observed how his body was laid.' They prepared spices and returned to the tomb on the first opportunity after the Sabbath and found no body. When they went to tell the apostles, the men would not believe them. How do you think the women felt about this? Why were the men conspicuous by their absense? Could you write a woman disciple's account of the Easter story?

There is more variety than one might expect in the Bible's images of God. In the first chapter of Genesis we read that both women and men were created in the image of God. However, the early part of the Israelites' story is one of hostility to female images of God. In spite of attempts to define the God of the Old Testament in line with the social organisation, some of the female divine attributes rooted in ancient tradition have survived. They are particularly notice-able in the wisdom literature. Three important Hebrew words used to describe God all have a female gender, and carry with them female associations. They are 'ruah', 'hokmah', and 'shekinah'.

'Ruah', meaning wind or breath, is used to describe the spirit of God. So when the world was created, and, accord-ing to Genesis 1:2 with 'a mighty wind that swept over the surface of the waters,' or in the alternative translation 'the spirit of God brooding over the surface of the waters'. The idea of spirit as implying a female aspect of God continued until at least the second century AD.

'Hokmah', or 'sophia' in Greek, meaning wisdom, is a female image of God found frequently in the Bible. The Wisdom of Solomon contains many such passages. Jesus is reported to have referred to wisdom as female: 'But wisdom is proved right by all her children.' (Luke 7:35)

Other writers, such as John and Paul, took over the wisdom idea and changed it into 'logos', which became masculine; Paul describes Jesus as 'the wisdom of God' in I Corinthians 1:24.

'Shekinah' originally meant dwelling or resting, but came to represent the presence of God, and took on a numinous connotation, the glory of the presence of God on earth. She is found in the Rabbinic literature as an alternative to God's name, for example in Deuteronomy 12:5, God's tabernacle (Leviticus 26:11) and God's face (Numbers 6:25). In the Haggadah, shekinah is associated with ruah hakodesh, the Holy Spirit, and with bath kol, the daughter of the voice, all female aspects of God indicating the presence of God in the world and God's closeness to humanity. In the New Testament the identification of shekinah with Christ is suggested in several Pauline letters (for example Colossians 1:27) and in much of John's gospel.

A further set of female aspects of God can be found in the bird imagery common to both Old and New Testaments. Perhaps the best known example is in the words of Jesus: 'O Jerusalem ... how often I have longed to gather your children together as a hen gathers her chicks under her wings.' (Luke 13:34)

Similar themes occur in the Psalms: 'Hide me in the shadow of your wings.' (Ps. 17:8) 'Both high and low among men find refuge in the shadow of your wings.' (Ps. 36:7) 'I will take refuge in the shadow of your wings until the disaster is past.' (Ps. 57:1) 'He will cover you with his feathers, and under his wings you will find refuge.' (Ps. 91:4)

Yet other passages refer to the essentially female activity of birth: 'I have stilled and quietened my soul, like a weaned child with its mother.' (Ps. 131:2) 'You forsook the creator who begot you and cared nothing for God who brought you to birth.' (Deut. 32:18, NEB) 'But Zion said ... "the Lord has forgotten me." Can a mother forget the baby at her breast, and have no compassion on the child she has borne?' (Isa. 49:14, 15) 'As a mother comforts her child, so I will comfort you.' (Isa. 66:13) 'Listen to me, O house of Jacob ... you whom I have upheld since you were conceived, and have carried since your birth.' (Isa. 42:3)

Topics for Further Discussion

1. Look again at the questions posed at the beginning of this chapter. Have your reactions changed in any way?
2. How far can we reconstruct tradition to include both female and male images of God? Try working through your usual Sunday worship service, altering it to include specifically female images of God and images of women and women's experience.
3. Mary Daly wrote, 'When God is male, male is God.' What did she mean? Do you agree?
4. Our relationship with God as Lord or Father is often described in terms of domination and subjection. What other ways of describing our relationship with God are suggested by other images of God, for example, light, sustainer, comforter, companion?

Humour as a Healing Agent

Humour can be an important agent in healing. The ability to laugh at ourselves and to see the funny side of situations which may otherwise oppress us, is a God-given gift and means of liberation. The following sketches are included for this purpose. Wherever they have been read publically, they have been used in this way. They are not intended to be taken literally or to cause offence.

God and Man and Woman

(This can be read by two people standing apart, allowing for pauses for thought and laughter as appropriate.)

A : In the beginning, God made man.
    He was so disappointed that he tried again,
    And the next time, he made woman.

B : EVE, THE FIRST WOMAN, WAS A VEGETARIAN.
SHE LIKED APPLES, AND ATE THE WRONG ONE.
MEN HAVE BEEN SUSPICIOUS OF VEGETARIANS EVER
SINCE.

A : Noah didn't eat apples.
He was a man . . . so he drank alcohol.
In fact, he drank so much alcohol that one day his sons
found their old man completely sozzled and lying in the
nude.
Women have been suspicious of alcohol ever since.

B : LOT DIDN'T EAT APPLES OR DRINK WINE.
HE JUST LIVED IN A CITY WHERE THE MEN DIDN'T
KNOW WHO THEY FANCIED.
SO GOD TOLD HIM TO LEAVE THE CITY, AND SO HE
DID.
GOD SAID, 'DON'T LOOK BACK, FOR I'M GOING TO
BURN DOWN THE CITY.'
SO LOT DIDN'T LOOK BACK, BUT HIS WIFE DID AND
SHE TURNED INTO A PILLAR OF SALT.
WOMEN HAVE NEVER LOOKED BACK SINCE.

A : Delilah didn't eat apples, drink wine or look back.
She was a hairdresser.
Samson didn't know that,
    but while he was resting his macho muscles,
    Delilah cut his hair and took his strength away.
Men have avoided being bald ever since.

B : ST. PAUL DIDN'T KNOW EVE, NOAH, LOT OR DELILAH.
BUT HE DID KNOW SOME WOMEN,
    AND THOSE HE DID MUST HAVE GIVEN HIM BAD
MEMORIES.
BECAUSE HE TOLD THEM NOT TO SPEAK IN CHURCH,
    NOT TO GO INTO A CHURCH WITHOUT A HAT
    AND ALWAYS TO OBEY THEIR HUSBANDS.
PAUL ALSO SAID THAT MEN SHOULDN'T GET
MARRIED UNLESS THEY WERE UNABLE TO CONTROL

THEMSELVES.
MEN HAVE BEEN UNABLE TO CONTROL THEMSELVES
EVER SINCE.

A : But Jesus was different.

He was strong, but he cried.
He even cried in front of other men.
He knew that some women had bad reputations,
    but that didn't keep him back from them:
He knelt beside them.

He loved his disciples who were all men
    and he wasn't afraid to tell them that he loved them.
And though he was never married,
    he was always surrounded by women who, at his
    death,
    were more faithful to him than the men.

Jesus didn't make a fuss about who was who or who was
what.
He said that everyone who loved him was his mother,
        his sister,
        his brother.

A&B: THANK GOD FOR JESUS.

He and She

This second script may be read by two people without
actions and preferably to a soft guitar or piano accom-
paniment. 'Summertime' is a particularly effective background tune.

A : He was the son of refugees.
    They hardly had time to circumcise him as a baby when
    the family had to go on the run.

B : SHE . . . WELL, NOBODY REALLY KNEW HER PARENTS,
    BUT MOST FOLK SAID THEY CAME FROM THE
    COUNTRY.

A : At the age of 12, he ran away from his mother and father

– the kind of things a lot of boys that age do.
But he didn't run off to get away from adults.
He did it to get closer to them.

B : SHE WAS PROBABLY 14 WHEN SHE HAD HER FIRST
PERIOD . . . A BIT LATE IN COMPARISON WITH MOST
GIRLS TODAY, BUT STILL QUITE NORMAL.

A : There was a job waiting for him when he was old
enough.
He was an apprentice in the family business.
It was a sort of living-above-the-shop kind of existence.

B : IT WAS PROBABLY WHEN SHE WAS 17 – OR SO THEY
SAY, – THAT SHE BECAME PREGNANT.
IT CREATED SUCH A SCANDAL THAT SHE HAD TO
LEAVE HOME . . . SO THEY SAY . . . AND THEY ALSO SAY
THAT HER BOYFRIEND NEARLY LEFT HER WHEN SHE
TOLD HIM THAT THE BABY SHE WAS EXPECTING
WASN'T HIS.

A : He didn't get married.
The way his job developed, it would have been difficult.
He left home when he was 30 and then went down in
the estimation of the people who had known him since
he was a boy.

B : SHE HAD SEVERAL CHILDREN AFTER HER FIRST SON,
BOYS AND GIRLS.
HER HUSBAND DIED WHEN HE WAS STILL A YOUNG
MAN, SO SHE WAS LEFT DEPENDING ON WHAT HER
SONS COULD EARN IN ORDER TO BRING UP THE
FAMILY.

A : He was popular with women, but not because he was a
bachelor or a flirt. It was because they felt safe in his
company. Even the girls other people called sluts found
that he understood them, and didn't abuse them . . . and
that made a difference.

B : SHE NEVER REMARRIED.
SHE WATCHED HER CHILDREN GROW UP, THEN GROW AWAY.
BUT SHE WAS ALWAYS SURROUNDED BY YOUNG PEOPLE.
HER SON'S FRIENDS OFTEN LOOKED IN TO MAKE SURE THAT SHE WAS ALL RIGHT.

A : His life came to a sticky end.
He became involved with the wrong type of people.
He talked openly about things that upset the status quo.
He was a threat to respectable and religious folk.
So they used their connections and got rid of him.

At his death, he was naked as at his birth, though more people saw his public and private parts . . . and laughed.

B : SHE LIVED A LONG LIFE, BUT NOT WITHOUT ITS UPS AND DOWNS.
AFTER LOSING HER HUSBAND, SHE WAS PESTERED BY PEOPLE WHO WANTED TO TALK ABOUT HER FAMILY.
ONE OF THE BOYS HAD MADE A NAME FOR HIMSELF AND SHE SUFFERED BECAUSE OF HIS POPULARITY AND REPUTATION.

THEN CAME THE DAY WHEN SHE SAW WHAT NO WOMAN WOULD EVER WANT TO WITNESS . . .
SHE SAW THE CHILD WHO HAD SUCKED AT HER BREAST, WITH A FATAL WOUND IN HIS.
(Here any music stops)

A : His name was Jesus.

B : HER NAME WAS MARY.

9. Rape or Abuse Crisis Counselling

An increasing number of rape cases are being reported through the media daily. An estimated one in seven women are potential victims for rape or sexual abuse. In spite of this, the Church remains often unaware and ill-equipped to help women who are either potential or actual victims. Many women you meet will have experienced rape or sexual abuse at some point in their lives.

It is vital that you know what you are doing when counselling the abused, and that you have had counselling training. It is not a job for the inexperienced. These notes will *not* teach you how to do it and should not be taken as such, but are guidelines that may be helpful when coming into contact with rape and abuse victims.

Rape/abuse victims may be:

1. Frightened—of people, places, situations.
2. Angry—at themselves, at the world, at their assailant.
3. Confused—was it their fault? Why did it happen?
4. Hurt—in physical pain and in emotional pain.

You must never:

1. Say 'I know just how you feel'—you don't, even if you are a rape survivor; the victim will feel differently from you in many ways.
2. Imply that it is the victim's fault—this can cripple people emotionally.
3. Look shocked or horrified—if you can't help it, explain.

Say 'I'm sorry, I find this very upsetting,' and pause to recover.

4. Pry into what happened—if they want to tell you, they will.

5. Don't say 'God loves you', or other similar platitudes —the chances are that they know that, but it is not necessarily helpful at that moment.

6. Don't just pray with someone and assume that it will be all right—the roots of pain will be deep-seated and will probably need a lot of counselling.

7. Never divulge names or details to *anyone* without permission. To break trust is the worst thing you can do. Don't even tell anyone by asking them to pray for 'so-and-so'. The most you can say is 'Can you pray for me and a person I am counselling?' There is no need to say more; God already knows the details.

Please be aware that to be abused is a terrible experience. To be a Christian and be abused can make things more complicated. Common responses include: 'Why did God let this happen?' and 'I called out to God, but he didn't stop it.' I can't answer these questions, and I don't know anyone who can. But being a Christian *does* have advantages. We have God's love and healing power with us, to help us and the victim. Pray constantly, not only for guidance, but for the victim.

It is our duty as Christians, and as members of one family, to care for each other. 'So that there should be no division in the body, but that its parts should have equal concern for each other.' (I Cor. 12:25)

We have a part in helping to rebuild people, and enabling them to become whole and fulfilled within God's family. Victims can become survivors.

Reactions to Rape

Shame, guilt, helplessness and physical repulsion are just some of the common feelings of rape victims. Nightmares, sleeplessness, shock, depression and damaged relationships are some of the emotional ways in which they can suffer, too.

In addition to any medical care that may be needed, women who have been assaulted also need special emotional support to come to terms with their experience. The experience of psychiatrists and crisis centre counsellors who have worked with rape victims is that the sooner a woman can start to talk about her experience, the quicker she will be able to come to terms with it.

But for some women it is a long time before they feel able to admit to what happened; they may be prompted to speak out finally by reports of other assaults. Many never tell—and live with a secret hurt for the rest of their lives.

Rachel Morris

PART III

RESOURCES

1. Addresses

Mothers and Toddlers

Pre-school Playgroup Association
General Secretary
Jane Atkinson
Alford House
Aveline Street
London SE11 5DH

Ministry to Young Mothers
CPAS Mission at Home
Falcon Court
32 Fleet Street
London EC47 1DB

Self-employed Women at Home

Bumpsadaisy is one way for young Christian mothers to reach others, as many of the existing franchisees have found, even though this isn't its primary reason for existence! For women at home with small children, or for those wanting to work part time and fit in business around a family, it offers a flexible way of meeting people and working without having to go out or find baby sitters. It can be run by an individual or by two or three working together to increase its potential. There are now over one hundred branches throughout Britain.

Starting a Bumpsadaisy

Bumpsadaisy is a franchise company with branches nation-wide. The franchisees are usually mothers, who have their showrooms at home. To join the franchise you need to:

1. Have a nice home with a room suitable for a showroom with space for a dress rail.
2. Have a telephone.
3. Have about £1,400 to invest in your business.
4. Know other young mothers and mothers-to-be in the area and be prepared to spend time visiting groups such as Mothers and Toddlers or ante-natal groups.
5. Have the energy to put time and effort into the business—but it's worth it!
6. Have a desire to meet people and help them by offering this service to mothers-to-be.
7. Be able to open your home to others and welcome them in.
8. Have the patience to deal with difficult customers—and with chaos if everything happens at once!
9. Like clothes, people and having something to do apart from your family!

For details of the Bumpsadaisy franchise, please contact

Penny Swithinbank
Department WTW
Bumpsadaisy
77 Ronalds Road
London N5 1XB

Involvement for the Full-time Housewife

For futher details about Prayer Triplets and Light in Every Street, contact:

Evangelism Department
Evangelical Alliance
186 Kennington Park Road
London SE11 4BT

Going it Alone

The Christian Friendship Fellowship arranges holidays and houseparties, local fellowship groups and friendship contacts for single believers. The address is

Christian Friendship Fellowship
Edenthorpe
Doncaster
South Yorkshire DN3 2QD

The Christian Friendship Introduction Service provides Christians who are looking for friendship and marriage with a means of contacting others. The address is

Christian Friendship Introduction Service
17 Church Road
Upton
Wirral
Merseyside L49 6JZ

Oak Hall organises many holidays for single Christians, specialising in skiing. The address is

Oak Hall Expeditions and Skiing
The Oaks
Tupwood Lane
Caterham
Surrey CR3 6DB

Single Parents

CLASP
Christine Tuffnell
Linden
Shorter Avenue
Shenfield
Brentwood
Essex CM15 8RE   Tel: 0227 233848

National Council for One Parent Families
225 Kentish Town Road
London NW5 2LX   Tel: 01 267 1361

Divorce Conciliation and Advisory Service
38 Ebury Street
London SW1 0LU   Tel: 01 730 2422

National Marriage Guidance Council
Herbert Gray College
Little Church Street
Rugby CV21 3AP   Tel: 0788 73241

The Gingerbread Association
35 Wellington Street
London WC2E 7BN   Tel: 01 240 0953

Children's Legal Centre
20 Compton Terrace
London N1 2UN   Tel: 01 359 6251

Family Rights Group
6/9 Manor Gardens
Holloway Road
London N7 6LA   Tel: 01 263 4016/9724
                   01 272 7308 for telephone advice sessions
                   Monday, Wednesday and Friday mornings.

Parents Anonymous (for those who feel they might abuse their
children under stress)
9 Manor Gardens
London N7 6LA   Tel: 01 263 8918

Cruse (for widows)
126 Sheen Road
Richmond
Surrey TW9 1UR   Tel: 01 940 4818/9047

The Mothers' Union
Young Families Department
24 Tufton Steet
London SW1P 3RB   Tel: 01 222 5533

CARE Trust
21a Down Street
London W1Y 7DN   Tel: 01 499 5949

The Association of Separated and Divorced Catholics
The Holy Name Presbytery
8 Portsmouth Street
Manchester M13 9GB

Christianity and Feminism: Must We Choose?

Men, Women and God has a library and resources centre
which can be used by members, and also produces a
resources pack for churches and small groups who wish to
look at feminist issues from a Christian perspective. Details
of local feminist activities can usually be found at your local
library if not through the local women's centre itself. The
address for Men, Women and God is

Men, Women and God
St Peter's Vere Street
London W1

Women in Prison

Prison Fellowship
PO Box 263
London SW1 6HP

Reaching Young and Isolated Women

If you want to be involved in a youth club, you can contact
your local education authority youth service and ask for
details. Alternatively, those who wish to be involved with
clubs with specific Christian aims (but not necessarily
church youth clubs) should contact

Frontier Youth Trust
130 City Road
London EC1V 2NJ   Tel: 01 250 1966

West Indian Women

The Centre for Caribbean Studies
Caribbean House
Bridport Place
Shoreditch Park
London N1 5DS   Tel: 01 729 0986

Meeting Asian Women

CLC Asian Literature Department
51 The Dean
Alresford
Hampshire SO24 9BJ

In Contact Ministries works in the inner cities of Britain, and specialises in work among the Asian and other ethnic communities. Over the years it has been involved in a church-planting ministry. Its ministry is threefold: evangelism including running of missions, caring ministry and a training ministry; running conferences; and training courses both at the St Andrew's Centre and in churches throughout the country.

In Contact Ministries
St Andrew's Road
Plaistow
London E13 8QD

In most areas there are courses to teach Asian women English, and these can be found by getting in touch with your local education authority.

Women in the Arts

The Arts Centre Group
21 Short Street
London SE1 8LT

Rape Crisis

If you know someone who is the victim of a sex attack, she can turn for advice and support to:

London Rape Crisis Centre	Tel: 01 837 1600
Birmingham Rape Crisis Centre	Tel: 021 233 2122
Manchester Rape Crisis Centre	Tel: 061 228 3602
Edinburgh Rape Crisis Centre	Tel: 031 556 9437

In addition, one of these centres may be able to put you in touch with one nearer your home.

General

Christian Women's Information and Resources has a library and useful catalogue. Members may borrow books by post. The address is

Christian Women's Information and Resources
c/o Blackfriars
St Giles
Oxford OX1 3LY

The Christian Women's Resource Centre sells books and has a catalogue. The address is

Christian Women's Resource Centre
36 Court Lane
Dulwich
London SE21 7DR

Two London bookshops which usually have a selection of books on feminist theology and will send books by post are:

Sisterwrite
190 Upper Street
London N1

Compendium Books
240 Camden High Street
London NW1

The British Council of Churches has some useful material and also stocks World Council of Churches publications. The address is

The British Council of Churches
2 Eaton Gate
London SW1W 9BL

2. Selected Bibliography

(NCOPF: National Council for One Parent Families)

Bailey. *The Ministry of Love and Marriage.* SCM.

Bainton, R.H. *Sex, Love and Marriage.* Collins/Fontana.

Bell, Hannah. *Pierced to the Heart.* Pickering & Inglis, 1984.

Bennington, John. *Culture, Class and Christian Beliefs.* Scripture Union.

Brackenbury Crook, M. *Women and Religion.* Beacon Press, 1964.

Brooks, Ira V. *Another Gentleman to the Ministry.*

Clark. *Man and Woman in Christ* (2 Vols). Servant.

Cook, D. *Are Women People Too?* Grove Booklet on Ethics, 21.

Coote and Jill. *Women's Rights.* Penguin.

Dejong-Wilson. *Husband and Wife.* Zondervan.

Derrick, Deborah (ed.). *Illegitimate: The Experience of People Born Outside Marriage.* NCOPF.

Dodgeon, Brian. *Making Family Allowances.* NCOPF.

Donoghue, Joyce. *Running a Mother and Toddler Club.* Unwin.

Dowling, Collette. *The Cinderella Complex.* Fontana.

Downing, A.B. *The Downing Flavour.*

Elliott, Elizabeth. *Let Me Be a Woman.* Tyndale.

Evans, Mary. *Woman in the Bible.* Paternoster.

Evans, Richard. *The Feminists.* Croomhelm, Barnes & Noble.

Fathers Alone: aspects of male lone parenthood. NCOPF.

Fiorenza, E.S. *In Memory of Her.* SCM, 1983.

Fletcher, H. and Dodson, J. *No Accountability, No Redress.* NCOPF.

Foh, Susan. *Women and the Word of God*. Presbyterian & Reform Publishing Co.

Friedan, Betty. *The Second Stage*. Abacus.

Fryer, Peter. *Stay in Power*.

Give Us a Break: Leisure Opportunies for Lone Parents. NCOPF.

Graham-Dixon, Sue. *Never Darken My Door: Working for single parents and their children 1918–1978*. NCOPF.

Graham Hall, Jean. *A Unified Family Court*. NCOPF.

Greer, Germaine. *The Female Eunuch*. Paladin.

——. *Sex and Destiny*. Secker & Warburg.

Itzin, Catherine. *Tax Law and Child Care*. NCOPF.

Jewett, P. *Man as Male and Female*. Eerdmans.

Julian of Norwich. *Revelations of Divine Love*. Penguin.

Katoppo, Marianne. *Compassionate and Free*.WCC.

Kuhns. *Women in the Church*. Herald Press.

Langley, Myrtle. *Equal Woman*. Marshall.

Lees, Shirley (ed.). *When Christians Disagree: The Role of Women*. IVP.

Letts, Penny. *Double Struggle*. NCOPF.

Lewis, C.S. *The Four Loves*. Fontana.

Maidment, Susan. *Child Custody: What Chance for Fathers?* NCOPF.

Malcolm, Kari Torjesen. *Women at the Crossroads*. IVP.

McPhee, Arthur. *Friendship Evangelism*. Kingsway.

Moss, Basil and Rachel. *Humanity and Sexuality*. Church House.

Oakley, Ann. *Subject Women*. Fontana.

Otwell, John H. *Sarah Laughed*. Westminster Press, Philadelphia.

Pape, Dorothy. *God and Women*. Mowbray.

——. *God's Ideal Woman*. IVP USA.

Parvey. *The Community of Women and Men in the Church*. WCC.

Perrier, Adelia. *Fuel Poverty: Case Studies from One Parent Families*. NCOPF.

Phoenix, Sybil. *Willing Hands*. Bible Reading Fellowship.

Radford Reuter, Rosemary. *Sexism and Godtalk*. SCM.

Ramsey, Paul. *One Flesh*. Grove Booklet.

Rendall, Jane. *The Origins of Modern Feminism*. Mowbray.

Richards, Janet Radcliffe. *The Sceptical Feminist*. Pelican.

Rogers, Rick. *Children, Separation and Divorce: How Schools Can Help*. NCOPF.

Russell, L.M. *Human Liberation in a Feminist Perspective*. Westminster Press.

Scanzoni and Hardesty. *All We're Meant to Be*. Word Books Texas.

Schaeffer, Edith. *Affliction*. Hodder & Stoughton.

Simpson, Robin, *For the Sake of the Children*. National Consumer Council.

Southwell, M. and Rose, H. *Pregnancy, Maternity and Education*. NCOPF.

Stag, Evelyn and Frank. *Women in the World of Jesus*. St Andrew Press.

Steinem, Gloria. *Outrageous Acts and Everyday Rebellions*. Flamingo.

Storkey, Elaine. *What's Right with Feminism*. SPCK.

Swidler, Leonard. *Biblical Affirmations of Woman*. Westminster Press.

Tompson, Betty. *A Chance to Change Women and Men in the Church*. WCC.

Tournier, Paul. *The Gift of Feeling*. SCM.

Townsend, Anne. *Single-handed*. Kingsway, 1985.

Walwin, James. *Passage to Britain*.

Whyte, William H. *The Organisation Man*. Penguin.

Wiersbe, Warren. *When Bad Things Happen to God's People*. IVP.

Women. *The Directory of Social Change*. Wildwood House.

Working Group. *Man Woman*. Ecumenical Youth Council (EYC Europe).